the Forty One

a story of hope and a car

BLU SANDERS

Title and car drawings: Jamie Mixon

for my brave father

As I read a bit about the year 1941, I realize rather quickly that I don't really know much about 1941. I've not read any of the books. I've never seen *Citizen Kane*. And despite the fact that my father watches the military channel incessantly (like as I type this), I can't tell you a whole helluva lot more than the basics about WWII, if that. But 1941, to me, really isn't about Pearl Harbor. It isn't about Hitler. It isn't about airplanes. It isn't about war at all. 1941, to me, is about a relic. A relic that sits in an unfinished, two-car garage with no garage doors, next to an old storage shed, beside a pecan tree, in the back of our backyard. 1941 is about four decades of dust. It's about finishing what you start. It's about running out of time. It's about learning. It's about family. And it's about love.

See, in this unfinished garage with no doors sit many things that will likely never be used again but will never be discarded. A few times over the years my father has used one miscellaneous thing (electrical wire, for example, or a copper pipe) and that has justified a lifetime of never throwing anything away. For years right by the side door of our house sat a broken toilet.

"I paid good money for that toilet," my father once told me.

And don't doubt it. It was a great toilet.

My father grew up poor. His mother, once left to an orphanage by her own father after her mother died, had a seventh grade education and worked as a cafeteria lunch lady in her later adult life after my grandfather passed away. My grandfather, who I never had the privilege to meet, worked in the produce business with my grandmother's father. My grandmother would tell stories of herself as a young girl carrying home grocery bags from their store full of the day's cash during the great depression, because even in times of despair, everybody had to eat. Even by today's standards my great-grandfather was wealthy. But, alas, he was an Arab. And back then in an Arab family the men got the money. My grandmother's brothers were rich. She and her three sisters never saw a penny.

Perhaps this meager upbringing led my father to develop his appreciation of craft and quality. My father has always preferred the best if the best was available. But if the best wasn't available, he'd build the best. Our bathrooms are all made, by his hand, with exquisite marble. Our kitchen cabinets are beautiful cherry wood with dovetailed drawers. Almost everything in our house he's designed and built himself. His tools are top notch. Hell, his razors are top of the line. Because you get what you pay for. And if there was a man who exemplified getting what you pay for, that man was my father. And if there was a man who exemplified not throwing away what you pay for, well that man was also my father.

And so, in the unfinished doorless garage sits a prized possession, next to a broken down John Deere tractor that will never run again, alongside maybe twenty used paint rollers in ten empty buckets, a box full of CD jewel cases from CDs that are long gone, an old office desk on its side, bunk beds, television boxes from televisions we don't own anymore, paint cans, tile, half a pitching machine, baseballs, hubcaps, fan belts, computer parts, bags of cement, brick ties, a drill press, duffle bags, my old skateboard, golf clubs, ladders, coolers, and well, that's just what I can see. Deep inside the unfinished doorless garage sits a prized possession camouflaged so well that if you didn't know it was there, you might even miss the 1941 Chevrolet suicide four door Special Deluxe.

Here's a typical morning in my new life. I wake up and come downstairs somewhere between 6:30 and 7:30 in the morning. My stepmother, Babette, is always up before I am. She's making coffee or working in her office. She owns a small mail advertising business with her brother and works out of the house. My father sleeps through the espresso machine. My father can sleep through just about anything. A vacuum. Doorbells. Dog barks. Anything. I come into the kitchen and make my first of two lattes – with sugar, to my father's dismay.

"You're ruining that coffee!" he insists each and every time I drink one.

Then I shuffle into the dining room where I've set up my indefinitely-temporary computer desk (plastic table). Underneath the table is an effects pedal board for my electric guitar that hasn't left its case since I've been home. Against the wall sits my Martin D-28 acoustic guitar, which I bought in college with my student loan in 1994, and have picked up maybe once since I got home. Two camera bags. One that holds my current digital Nikon and the other that holds my first digital Nikon that my father bought me for my birthday several years before and I sent back to him after I moved up to a newer one only to find out that he couldn't actually use the camera because he couldn't push the buttons with his weak fingers.

I check my email. Tech news. Facebook. Twitter.

When I get downstairs Babette switches places with me and goes upstairs to take a shower. I sleep in their old bedroom. My father's legs have been too weak to go up the stairs for nearly a year. And the year before that it took so long each time he tried to do it that he eventually just quit trying.

And so now they sleep downstairs in the room where my father first slept when he bought this house in 1972, before he added a second story, and when he was married to my mother. That room still decorated with flowery pastel yellow wallpaper like my twin sister left it when she went to college almost twenty years ago. Moving downstairs was another surrender for my father. It was a small defeat on a long list of defeats in a futile attempt to beat the unbeatable.

Then I hear my dad moving in the baby monitor that sits on my desk. Usually a yawn or a stretch or a "Yoo hoo!" and I know he's ready to get out of bed. He told me sometimes he's scared that no one will hear him. No one will come. And he'll just lie in bed. Alone. Unable to do anything.

I walk from the new part of the house to the old part of the house and down the hall into his bedroom. Roll him from his side onto his back. Reach behind his shoulders and pull him up like an anchor to a sitting position. Then turn him to hang his legs off the bed. Pull him closer to the edge. Wrap around him once more. Rock him back and forth, and lift him up into a sort of half-stance slumped over me like a rag doll and by some sort of an awkward slow dance, over into his wheelchair that I have positioned next to his bed. His body is weak in the mornings. What's left of it is waking up. Some days it doesn't seem like it'll wake up at all. I straighten him up in the chair and like clockwork give him a urinal. He can only piss in a urinal now because he can't stand at a toilet anymore. And if someone isn't there to help within maybe thirty seconds he'll just piss on himself. He finishes and I take the urinal and empty it into the toilet down the hall. Then I go back and place his hand on the wheelchair joystick and he drives himself down the hall and into the living room. He can still use the joystick on his wheelchair.

By this time Babette's downstairs again. One of us makes my dad a latte (no sugar) with a straw. My father's hands can't really squeeze and pick up a glass anymore. Then he rolls himself up to his computer. I put the coffee on his desk and he leans over to take a sip. Sometimes from behind you think maybe he's fallen face first into his desk, but he's just drinking coffee.

Then with his left hand he lifts his right hand onto the computer mouse. And then with his left hand he moves his right hand. Misclicks. Triple-clicks. Moves the mouse all over the goddamn screen in a long laborious effort just to look at the news. He spends hours upon hours on his computer surfing the web. Worldofwatches.com where he can buy watches he can't even put on his own wrists. Newegg.com for computer parts he can't assemble. Wood working videos about wood he will never work again. Over and over and fucking over again day after day after long silent day because there is nothing else in the world that he is truly capable of doing. I can't even begin to fathom the staggering boredom that has slowly overtaken his world.

Babette and my father got married just a few short years ago in the only ceremony I'd ever been to where the crowd cheered out loud at the nuptials as if they just scored a touchdown. Chock full of Babette's extended Syrian family, many, including me, thought it perhaps a long time coming. Babette was from El Paso and worked for my father in the eighties when my sister, brother, and I were kids. But even when she moved clear across the country for fifteen years, she treated my sister, my brother, and me like her own. After we were all grown and gone, she came back to El Paso to care for her father, reacquainted with mine, and married into a commitment beyond what anyone could reasonably guess a commitment might entail.

I don't know how she ever did any of it alone. From the simplest task that only needed to be remembered, to getting my father in and out of the shower, I just don't know how she actually did it. My father weighs somewhere near two hundred and ten pounds. That's like lifting a two hundred and ten pound bag of water. Shifting. Moving. Offering vanishing help with what strength he has left in his legs. His arms offer a bit of balance, but it's mostly you and his body and I don't know how a small woman could have done it.

Babette eventually called and asked that I come home. My father had gotten worse, she said, and she couldn't do it by herself anymore. Now, coming home to care for my father was a tomorrow I always knew would come, but I just never knew when it would come. But like all tomorrows do, eventually, it came.

My father was diagnosed with the neuromuscular disease Amyotrophic Lateral Sclerosis (ALS), also known as Lou Gehrig's disease in 2006, almost four years ago.

Lou Gehrig was a professional baseball player in the 1930s. He had an exemplary career with the New York Yankees until he died tragically at the young age of thirty-seven. He was an All-Star, an MVP, a Triple Crown Winner, and an ALS victim.

Technically what happens when you get ALS is that the motor neurons that control your muscles die. As they die, nerves fire randomly. Watching my father is like watching a hundred muscle spasms at the same time. His cheeks quiver. His thighs. His arms. His back.

After they die, the brain can no longer control muscle movement. You are slowly imprisoned in your own body. You lose your ability to walk. To use your hands. You cannot feed yourself. You cannot bathe yourself. You cannot speak. You cannot swallow. You cannot breathe. You suffocate or you starve to death. You can't even kill yourself.

ALS is a death sentence. The cause and cure remain unknown. There is no real treatment. If you get ALS you will not survive. But how the disease starts and how long it lasts varies from person to person. It started in my father's right foot. It may start in your foot, or it may start in your arm. Or if you're unlucky you'll have a bulbar onset and you immediately won't be able to talk, or even worse, a respiratory onset, and your breathing will go first. My father says he didn't even realize he had a problem until someone at the courthouse pointed out that he was limping. But who thinks you have a fatal disease when you have a little bump in your step?

They call ALS a diagnosis of exclusion. That is, once they've ruled everything else out, that's what you've got. There is no test, per se. So I suppose there is always the thought in the back of our heads that maybe my father actually has something else. That there was a mistake and maybe he really has MS, or Guillain-Barré, or something manageable with a difficult name. And that one day he'll walk again. He'll use his hands again. But that's only a hope. And hopes don't really make you walk again.

ALS is a rare disease we are told. But the more you talk about it the less rare it seems. I first learned about it from a friend whose husband was diagnosed at the rare age of twenty-eight. I went to both his wedding and his funeral in a few short years. The father of a girl at my last job has ALS. Another friend's father was recently diagnosed. But ALS is a rare disease we are told.

Four years ago is lucky it seems. People come and go with ALS and you never know quite how long it's gonna take. Over the years we've met the most people with the disease in clinics and support groups. Every three months in the first years after my father's diagnosis he went to a clinic in Houston. I would fly in and go with him when I could. They ran him through a laundry list of checkups. They monitored him. Told him, for example, how good or bad his breathing was compared to how it was three months prior. A pulmonologist might have told him his breathing was fine or they might have told him he needed oxygen. An occupational therapist might have told us how to use a lift to get my father up from the ground if he ever fell, or how to stretch his legs because he hardly used them anymore. Or if he was lucky he'd get into a clinical trial for a new drug that wouldn't work. It wasn't really treatment at the clinics so much as it was preparation. Here's what you're gonna need while you die, and here's how fast you're gonna need it. Clinics are studying you for their own research, with the ultimate hope of course, being a cure. But it wore on my father and eventually he decided to stop going.

"Your father is dying," he said to me. "What else are they gonna tell me?" And I couldn't really argue with that.

Even here in El Paso in our small support group, one day we'd go to the group and someone would be gone. Then a new person. Then they'd be gone. And it continues, and never stops.

In a sweet and heartbreaking show of solidarity at the first meeting I attended, my father and Mr. Martinez, a patient in our group, raised their arms as high as they could, which is to say they hardly raised their arms at all, and touched smooth muscle-less wrists because they didn't have the strength to shake hands.

"I waaaant tooo ruuuun iiiiin myyy yaaaard," Mr. Martinez said slowly like a sloth moves. "Buuuut I caaaan't. I'm oooookkkk uuuuup heeeere." He slowly pointed to his head. "Buuuut I'm noooot oooookkkk doooown heeeere." He slowly pointed to his legs.

"I know," acknowledged my father.

I remember when my dad called to tell me he had fallen in the courtroom as he walked in with a stack of folders in his hand. A prognosis of sorts. It didn't seem like much longer after that he was in a wheelchair at his retirement party.

My father, after growing up poor, working young, putting himself through college, joining the navy, going to law school, working his ass off, raising three kids, finding love again at sixty-three, and paying his house off, was finally happy. Finally happy. Retiring. And dying.

But to say there was no good fortune wouldn't be completely fair. After retirement my father's little red motorized wheelchair went everywhere from China to Key West. I drove him and Babette on a three week honeymoon RV trip to the Pacific Northwest. We watched whales in Alaska. Saw the Statue of Liberty. Played the penny slots in Vegas.

But then you forget about good fortune when your father is choking in the Cracker Barrel on his own saliva.

My dad still lives in the same house I grew up in. Sometime in the late seventies he, along with the same set of hard workers who have been helping him with projects for decades, added a second story addition to his and my mother's small one-story, three bedroom, one bathroom house. Paz could hammer nails into wood in one fierce pound. Pepe was fifteen when he came to work with my dad. He still comes by the house, now with his son Guero. Guero now with a son of his own. My father, often in shorts, a tool belt, no shirt, and wavy seventies hair, hunkily finished off the crew. And I still have the rusted old Tonka bulldozer that my dad bought me because I wanted one like the one that was moving dirt in the backyard.

Our house has always been a work in progress. As our lives are a work in progress maybe. But really, ours is. Until very recently it was as if our house was perpetually being worked on. From missing molding to a half built BBQ pit, to a deck with no decking, there always seemed to be something left to do.

Then ten years ago I bought a condo of my own. Not long after I bought the place I took a carpet knife to the Berber after a flood, tossed it out the back door and proceeded to work on it for the next eight years until I sold it, never once being satisfied, not even when I handed it off to the next owner. It seems that when you have the time to change your mind, you do. If you don't like red you can try blue. If you don't like tile you can try wood. And then you can change your mind again.

You make choices. What are the things that need to be done vs. what are the things that you want to be done, while you can do them, while you have time to do them?

If there is a next life, and I believe that there is a far greater chance of that than there is ascending into heaven to be reunited with Trey and Licorice our childhood standard poodles, then my father will most certainly be a general contractor.

But this knowledge seems to be generational. That is, people my age generally don't know shit about anything, and people my dad's age do. Some of that was born out of necessity. We don't have to change our own oil anymore. We can take our car to Jiffy Lube and thirty minutes later we have new oil. But my father was never happy unless he was doing something with his own hands, and in his defense, there was about a ninety-nine percent chance he did it better.

Some of this was also born out of culture. That is, people my dad's age didn't seem to be making some lazy wandering attempt at fulfilling their spiritual purpose, whereas I have been lazily wandering and attempting to fulfill my spiritual purpose for the better part of a decade.

Now, I've done a minor amount of manual labor over the years. I've changed my alternator, my brakes, pulled my radiator out once, laid tile, even built a counter top, but really all that was just due to budget and I've retained essentially no knowledge or tools from all the work I've ever done. At one point in my life I owned socket sets, handsaws, drills, routers, you name it. But they have all since disappeared and are presumably in an alternate universe with my lost guitar picks.

My dad, however, can do basically anything. He can put a sprinkler system in your yard, fix your air conditioner, design and build your kitchen shelves, or do your divorce, but I can promise you he would rather be sweating in the hot sun with a tool belt around his waist than sitting in front of a judge, which is one of the most tragic parts of his disease. To watch my father lose his hands, his ability to do the only things that have ever kept him sane or happy, could not be any more unjust.

The '41 was never a part of some special collection. It wasn't an investment or an heirloom passed down. It was just a project of my dad's that he always intended, but never got around, to finish. And so it sat for nearly forty years, never quite getting the attention it deserved, never driven, almost forgotten. It was the molding, the BBQ pit, the deck.

There was a time when I used to think that not finishing what you start, or even just starting something else, was a symptom of something dark. A crutch. A flaw. But I've come to realize that life is but a series of projects, and some projects are simply unfinished. That's the thing about projects. You always think you can go back and finish them. But that's just it. Sometimes you can't. Sometimes something happens that stops all of your projects.

And so today is the day. Today is the day I start to finish one of my father's projects. Today I start the molding, the BBQ pit, the deck. Today I fight for a win in the midst of total loss. A victory though guaranteed defeat. Today I begin to do whatever in the world I have to do to fix the '41 and take my father for a ride before he dies.

My name is Bluford Bradford Sanders III. Blu for short. Like the color, I tell anyone I'm introducing myself to, but not really. My father is also Blu, but my grandfather was called Buffalo for reasons no one really ever knew.

After high school I thought I left West Texas for good, but sometimes things just don't end up like you think they will. At thirty-five, in the spring of 2010, I left my life as a musician, songwriter, and sometimes photographer in Nashville, Tennessee and came home to the city where I was raised, El Paso, Texas. Hold your left hand up, palm facing you. Your hand is Texas. Point to the tip of your thumb. That's El Paso.

In the nineties after college I was a computer monkey in Austin, Texas, building databases and E-Commerce websites when E-Commerce was a buzzword and people were over-hired and over-paid. After being laid off when the tech bubble burst, I left Austin for New York City to "follow my dreams," some people might say, of making it in the music business. I soon found out that there were many ways and many, many degrees of making it in the music business.

When you're young, making it is what everyone thinks making it is. Touring. Being famous. Getting laid. When you're pushing forty and you've been handily rejected for fifteen solid years by just about everyone you've ever met in the music business, making it is more about desperately not going back to a cubicle. So in that respect, I suppose I've made it. I've lived the last decade or so scraping by as a musician. Emphasis on scraping.

I got a booking agent and a manager and toured colleges, mostly by myself, on what was called the "coffee house circuit" playing for whoever'd listen, lots of times no one, or whoever happened to be eating lunch in the school cafeteria. I slept on couches and such and stayed at America's dumpiest motels while criss-crossing the country often living out of my four banger truck with no cruise control, satellite radio, or GPS, gathering just enough fans (read: not many) to not quit. Spent every single penny I had. Quite literally paying my dues and then some.

About ten years ago a country artist named Jack Ingram recorded one of my songs for an album of his. Now, I had never really fancied myself a "songwriter" per se. I was writing songs, making records, and playing gigs just like any musician. I looked up the producer of the record in Nashville, caught a flight, knocked on his office door, and asked what I was supposed to do next. He told me I could hang my hat there at his publishing company when I was in town and they would help get me writing. I went every spare weekend I had off. I slept on the office couch. I showered at the Y. I wrote mostly mediocre country songs with other people just like me. After a couple years I was signed as a staff songwriter and made a thousand dollars a month. Nearly ten times less than my last year as a monkey.

Along the way I snapped photos with my father's cameras I'd inherited, or just kinda took, when I left home for college. There are old black and white photos of my father as a kid with a camera strapped around his neck. But he wasn't a professional photographer or anything like that. He was just a guy who loved photos and bought some good cameras. Occasionally I got paid to shoot photos of someone's kid. Cameras went completely digital. I shot a few weddings here and there. Some independent album covers. I learned that being creative in any way was truly the key to staying out of the cubicle. That was really making it. I got a small raise. I could pay cheap rent.

I started to work with a young act called the Eli Young Band out of Denton, TX. Four young good looking guys and a singer with a great country voice. We wrote songs. We travelled in a crappy family van. They graduated to a fifteen passenger van. Got popular. Moved to a bus. I started to play second guitar. It was the most fun I'd ever had playing music.

The band recorded two of my songs for their first major label album. One of them was even a single. It climbed the Billboard charts into the thirties until the record label pulled the plug on the album for mysterious record label reasons that my mother will never understand.

But when my father was diagnosed I was slowly unable to commit to just about everything, in anticipation of what was to come.

To be clear, writing songs for a living was amazing. It hurt sometimes, and it never paid too well, but it sure beat sitting in an office or weed whacking a golf course like I did that one summer in high school. But sometimes you forget who you are, trying to write songs for other people. Acting like someone else. In some ways, leaving helped me remember who I was.

Before I left Nashville I drove a decade's worth of my unsold CDs to the Nashville dump. I stood on the tailgate of my truck looking down into the giant garbage container at what must have been hundreds and hundreds of albums. My history. What I'd worked so hard for. It felt strange. Like failure in some ways. Like relief in others. But I couldn't fit the damn things in the trailer, so they had to go.

Since I was a kid I sat in the '41 and pretended it worked. Bounced up and down on the front seat. Drove it all over the universe in my young imagination. Brought my friends inside. Took trips with them. Was a limo driver. A rock star. Went to work. Just cruised. My brother and I talked for years about fixing it up, but like things do, it got put aside, or we never really made a plan, or whatever it was, and it never got done. Then sorta like a death at an intersection prompts an overdue traffic light, sometimes tragedy begets progress. That is, were I not home to care for my dad, the '41 would still be collecting dust in the garage.

But the "car" is only a shell. There is no engine. No transmission. No starter (I'm guessing). No nothing. It's a body, an interior, a frame, and wheels. The bumpers and running boards are on the ground underneath it. And that's the thing. I don't really have any idea how to restore a car. Where to start. How to finish. And everything in between. I need help. And there are two of my father's friends who I always consult for anything car related.

The first is John Attel. John happens to be Babette's cousin, but my father has known the Attels for as long as I can remember and probably a little bit before that. John looks like a slightly Arab Welcome Back Kotter, complete with the curly hair and spot-on mustache, is about the funniest motherfucker on the planet, and is the smartest car guy you never knew. Smarter than your dad, your brother, and all your car friends combined. When we have a car problem, we called John, and John is always right. He's an engineer by trade, worked for GM back in the day, and now runs a successful car dealership in town.

The second is Eddie Solis. Eddie is another longtime friend of my father's. There has always been John Attel and there has always been Eddie Solis. Eddie is a jovial, light skinned Mexican man, with a bit of a belly, and a full head of dark hair. He used to have a junkyard back in the eighties along the banks of the Rio Grande. Years ago Eddie and my father took the '41 apart to fix it up or rebuild the engine or something along those lines because the engine, my dad had always told me, "is in Eddie's garage." I started to think it was bullshit every time my dad would say it, because who in the world would keep someone else's engine in their garage for nearly thirty years? Well, Eddie Solis would. That's who.

Eddie sorta disappeared over the years. I remember him from when I was much younger. I remember going to his junkyard. I can still see it in my head on the river near the border. There are photographs of my dad and Eddie in Mexico City climbing the pyramids together. But then I don't really have a real recollection of Eddie for most of the middle of my life. Somewhere in the last five or six years he resurfaced and I'd see him on trips home and now it's like he never left.

I decide to call Eddie first, since Eddie has the engine, to explain to him what I want to do.

"Yessir. What can I do for you, Blu Two?" Eddie talks like a professor. Precisely. He calls me Blu Two, even though technically I'm Blu Three.

"Well, I wanna get the '41 running and basically have no idea how to do it."

Eddie laughs. "Alright then. What would you like to do first?"

"I don't really know where to start but my dad says that the engine is over in your garage, so I guess I'd like to come by and check it out." Seems like a good first step to me.

"It is indeed. In fact I've been wanting to get all the parts back to your father for a while now so you can have them there at the house in case you need them. But if it were me, I'd probably put something else in there, because the 216..."

I interrupt. "The original engine is a 216?" I ask like I know what a 216 is but not really having any idea what a 216 was.

"That's correct. And that was before engines had oil pressure. Instead of pressure, the engine had little spoons that came up to catch the oil and..." I lose him. None of this means much of anything to me. I imagine cartoon kitchen teaspoons on the engine turning a circle picking up a pool of oil and taking it to...the oil place on the engine?

"Pick a morning and you can come by and look at everything," he tells me.

"Ok perfect. I'll call you," and we hang up.

Eddie meets my dad, Babette, and me for breakfast on a morning at the Cracker Barrel near our house and I leave with him from the restaurant to go see the engine. Eddie lives in a small one-story brick house with a wrought iron fence around it and more concrete than grass for a yard, right across from the border highway, which is exactly what it sounds like—the highway that runs along the US-Mexico Border. His garage looks and smells like any garage that has been a garage for fifty years. Filled to the brim with a little bit of everything, and presumably only he knows where everything is. And sure enough, like a myth, sits the Chevy 216 stock engine for the '41 as if it hasn't moved an inch since the day he and my dad brought it over here so many years ago. My dad had said the '41 was driven to him when he first got it. It actually ran. But since then, the only thing

I know for sure is that the engine was taken out, never put back in, and it hasn't been driven since.

We talk a bit about the engine. Sorta like Charlie Brown talks to his teacher. "Now if we wanna stay original," Eddie tells me, "we use the 216. But if we want to make life easier, the best choice for a different engine for the '41 would be a 250. Those are also a straight six, so there is not major work to be done like there would be putting an eight cylinder engine in, for example, and there was a significant jump in progress between the two engines."

A straight six cylinder engine has six cylinders in the engine in a straight line one after the other, unlike a V8 engine, which has four cylinders on one side and four on the other in a V formation. I have no real idea how straight cylinders were really different or better than having them divided on each side, other than geometrically, or really how an engine works at all, so I just say, "If you say the 250, then let's do the 250."

I have no idea where to buy an engine.

In conversation, it comes up that we don't have a title for the car. My father got the '41 as a barter for a legal fee in the early seventies and there simply wasn't a title, or there was but it was lost, or who knew. So we decide that the first thing we need to take care of before we do any work on the car is to get a title. No sense in putting time and money into the car if, in the end, it's technically someone else's car. Eddie says that titling an older vehicle like this should be simpler than a new vehicle but that we need to go downtown and talk to the Tax Assessor's office to find out the process.

Eddie drives towards downtown and the Tax Assessor's office. We stop off on a quick errand at a rundown one-story office building where a little man named Harry, who I'm told owns many downtown

El Paso buildings, is standing on the corner waiting for Eddie. We get out, I'm introduced, and we walk into the building. Harry brings us into an empty office-looking room and asks Eddie, "Is this wall load bearing?" while knocking on it.

Eddie takes a good look. Walks around a bit. "It isn't," Eddie says. The man thanks him, and we're back on our way.

Just a few blocks away is the county court house. The county court house where my father worked as a Public Defender for the last eight years of his career and spent thirty more in and out as a private, defense and family, attorney after a brief practice in Houston after law school.

My father ran for Justice of the Peace in the seventies. I come across photos on occasion of me and my sister wearing matching "Vote for My Dad!" t-shirts standing on a street corner somewhere in El Paso. He had a short run as a municipal court judge, and was even deputized by the Sherriff early in his career. He later ran for District Judge in the nineties, a natural progression for an attorney. He lost both races, but always was, and continued to be, a long time El Paso Democrat who gave many years to the citizens of El Paso, worked often for free, and campaigned incessantly for Democratic candidates and causes.

I remember the District Judge campaign well. The "Vote Blu" posters. The goofy family photos with my dad lying in front of us kids with a fake smile in my uncle's giant yard. Election night. I can count on one hand the number of times I've seen my father cry. The first was when my older cousin Brent was hit by a one-ton dually pulling horses, breaking nearly every bone in his little sixth-grade body. My uncle called from the hospital to let us know what had happened and that the doctors didn't think my cousin would make it. Somehow Brent didn't die, but I've never forgotten watching my father pick up the phone and get the news. The second was sitting on the stairs outside my father's law office after the District Judge election results came in.

In 2003 he was offered a position as a public defender for El Paso County, a commendable job if there ever was one. For my dad it was like semi-retirement. He had an office. He had a decent, reliable paycheck. He had health insurance. He left at five. The work came to him and he didn't take it home. He loved everyone he worked with, and even better, he already knew everything. At times I think he wondered why he hadn't been a public defender for the thirty years before that.

So Eddie and I park in the same garage my father used to park in, and walk to the Tax Assessor's office where there's surprisingly no line, and head straight to a good-looking Latina blonde who tells us that to get a title for a car with no title we have to fill out a form, which she finds and hands us, and set up a hearing with a supervisor, which we can do after we fill out and return the form. It's quick and simple. Eddie drives me home.

It takes me all of five minutes actually to fill out the form, but a good two weeks to get it back to the Tax Assessor's office.

I avoid the interstate and drive on the border highway, as I do on many days, along the Rio Grande, towards downtown El Paso. On my left is ASARCO, our beloved smelter plant, which, in the process of smelting copper, poisoned our, New Mexico's, and Mexico's soil with lead. ASARCO closed and never reopened, despite, after a cleanup effort, their commercials on local TV suggesting that we were all but fools not to believe it was safe again. The smokestack still sits eight hundred and twenty-eight feet above the city dwarfed only by the Franklin Mountains just to the east.

The Franklins split El Paso in half. They are the end of the Rocky Mountains, The Franklins offer a sort of beacon to any traveler. If you don't know where you are in El Paso you just have to find the mountains and you can figure it out. While El Paso may not be regarded as the most beautiful city in the world, there is nothing quite like a rare dust of snow on the red and brown terrain in the middle of a desert winter.

And to my right what some people are calling the most dangerous city on earth, a shell of our sister city, Juarez, Mexico, where people can't even walk outside their own houses without fear of being gunned down for...walking outside their houses. Slaughtered in the most heinous of ways. Decapitated with their heads stuffed in igloo coolers or hung from a telephone pole so that we'd know who's boss. And we know. The drugs are boss.

On a recent trip downtown, the border highway was blocked by the Border Patrol as there was a gun fight just on the other side of the river. Some of the bullets actually hit UTEP, our city university.

Some people wonder when the violence is going to come to El Paso. Some people say it already has. Scary times for an otherwise safe city.

The border highway flows past the bus depots, border shopping foot traffic, billboards and store signs in Spanish, and into downtown El Paso. I find a meter and hustle into the Tax Assessor's office. Again, no line.

"Hi," I say to the girl at the counter, not the blonde. I hand my form to her with a quick explanation. "I'm trying to get a title for a car that doesn't have a title, and this is a Statement of Fact from my father, who is unable to come in to the office because he is disabled."

She walks the form over to another woman who then joins her at the counter.

"Is this the form you were told to fill out?" the new woman asks me.

I explain that indeed it was the form I was given last time I came in. I tell her briefly about the '41 to make it a little more personal. "I just don't wanna do too much work before I have the proper paperwork."

"Do you have the VIN?"

I pull out my phone and read her a number I'd entered into it. "X24AP." I had found that number on the inside of the driver's side door frame, but wasn't really sure it was the VIN. But they didn't stamp a VIN on a sticker on the dash like they do nowadays and it was the only thing I could find that looked close. She writes it down and looks it up on the computer at the counter. "Nothing," she says. "No VIN. Do you have any paperwork for the car?"

"No," I answer. "No paperwork. No title. That's why we're filling out this form I thought."

"Well, you may have the wrong form," she explains. "And your father will have to come in at some point so that we know he is who you say he is."

I sort of sigh for effect. "Ok," I say, not really sure if he'll ever actually be able to come in. I hand her my and my father's IDs and she steps away to make copies. I take a seat in the lobby and call Eddie to tell him I think we have the wrong form.

The woman motions me to another station. I hang up the phone. "Do you have the original motor in the car?" she asks me.

"Well yes and no," I say. "I have the original motor but it's not actually in the car."

"It's not in the car?"

"It's not in the car."

"Well, the car has to be running to get a title."

"Really?" I say, surprised. "I didn't know that." And am pretty sure that isn't correct. She steps away to get a book of forms, sets the book down, and thumbs through the various forms with me.

There are title forms for replicas for which you needed a manufacturer's certificate, a rebuilt affidavit, a pencil tracing of the frame number. There's one for assembled vehicles using a manufactured prefabricated body. We read through a few more forms and eventually decide the correct form is form 67B, application for assigned or reassigned number, which was the form I got in the first place, had filled out, and handed to her when I walked in.

With that she says, "Now you have to make an appointment and take the car to VIN Inspections with the first half of 67B filled out. They'll find the VIN on the motor, or on the frame, and fill out the other half of the form. Then you'll bring back the entire completed form to me, at which point you request a hearing to get the title assigned. At this hearing I will reject this claim and send it to a judge across the street. The judge across the street will ok the title at which point you come *back* to the tax assessor and they can approve your request. Then you pay the tax title and license fees."

She doesn't really tell me where VIN Inspections is and I don't really ask but I take the form (again), thank her, and am on my way. I leave more or less about as unsure as I went in, but thinking I might have made some progress, though not totally sure.

I stop into Home Depot to pick up some thirty-six-inch left-handed exterior metal doors, and then head home to fill out form 67B for a second time.

One of the advantages to living in the same city your entire life is that you know everybody. Your buddy in elementary school ran the newspaper. Your next door neighbor now had three car dealerships. So and so had been a judge since the seventies. And on and on. Not that being anywhere for forty-plus years didn't result in similar relationships, but these days everyone was doing everything and at a younger age and there were just lots more people in lots more places. You probably didn't kick around town when there was no town. You didn't have a story about driving home from law school and seeing LBJ and his caravan of only two other cars blow by you in a convertible, but my dad did. And being in the legal business for forty years had resulted in its own set of relationships, and many long lasting friendships.

My father's friend Victor Flores is now the Tax Assessor for El Paso County, so my dad has me call Victor. And like I did most times those days, I leave a message that this is the son of Blu Sanders, Little Blu, and that I'm calling for my father because unfortunately he isn't able to talk very well, and that we are trying to title an old car and are unsure what to do.

When Victor calls I put the phone on speaker and my father and Victor make jokes about the Army (Victor was in the Marines. My dad the Navy). He asks how my father is. My dad struggles to tell him in a voice that he can hear. Mostly I translate for him. I tell Victor about the car and Victor tells us he'll send a VIN inspections officer to our house to inspect the '41 since my dad can't make it downtown with the car. He says there's a process and this will kick start the process and we'll go from there.

"See?" my dad looks at me and tells me without actually saying anything.

"Yeah, I shoulda called Victor in the first place."

The thirty-six-inch doors I bought are for the handicap bathroom that we're building. Metal because my father likes the durable metal doors and thirty-six inches because standard doors are thirty-two inches. Two extra inches on each side feel like a foot on either side of a completely different door. We're knocking down a wall and changing a tiny bathroom and small office into a big wide open bathroom with a roll-in shower. A roll-in shower is an absolute must for an ALS patient yet is sadly rare since it requires both the room for it and a budget. You can get by on suction cup handles on the shower walls until you can't grab them anymore and then maybe with a shower chair, but when your legs start to go, a six-inch step into a shower might as well be a brick wall.

Now I say "we" loosely. I basically stand around like a fool with my iPhone translate app and "talk" to Carlos, the big block of a Mexican worker who comes over the bridge, like so many workers do in El Paso, and does pure raw labor for more money than probably anyone has paid him in his life, but perhaps for not much considering the actual work involved. (This is the part where you talk about immigrants and how they take people's jobs. And then you remember how you won't come over and do back breaking work for anything less than...well for anything.)

"Como se dice este?" The most frequent Spanish question I ask. *How do you say?*

"Desague." *Drain.*

"Y este?"

"Ladrillos." *Tile.*

"Ah. Ladrillos. Quieres comida?" *Do you want something to eat?*

"Sí."

"Ok." While Carlos breaks concrete with a sledgehammer with a big ol' smile on his face and my father sleeps right through it.

I did a bit of work in the last bathroom my dad and Babette remodeled, but this time around my job is basically to go to Home Depot four times a day and come back with the wrong things.

I get my father up out of bed to have a look at the progress. We stop for a snack in the kitchen where my father chokes on watermelon, about the most innocuous thing you could consume next to maybe water. Every choking episode seems like certain death. Gasping for breath. Holding his arms in the air and pounding on his back while food and spit run down his face and all over his shirt.

My father got a feeding tube just before I came home in anticipation of needing it down the line. That's what they told us to do. Don't wait until you need it they said. There are two major choices to make with ALS. One is whether or not you want a machine to breathe for you when you can no longer breathe on your own, and the second is whether or not you want a feeding tube after you can no longer swallow your food. Forgoing one meant a sooner death. My father chose a feeding tube. It was a relatively simple, albeit painful, surgery and he got used to having a tube poking out his gut. He would show it to friends and give us an occasional laugh by an, "Ahhhh!" of relief when we'd run water through the tube to clean it.

About five years ago my father was appointed the public defender on a DWI case for a young man named Willie. This was Willie's third DWI. He had a drug bust when he was younger, and that combined with another DWI meant he was going to jail. Willie had a long scar across the entire right side of his head, jaw, and into his mouth from the many surgeries it took to repair it after his uncle shot him in the face as a child.

But three times does seem like too many times. Luckily, Willie never hurt anyone but himself. At the time he was working as a cabinet maker for a company in El Paso, where they paid their laborers eight dollars an hour to build cabinets in a warehouse with no air conditioning in a climate that regularly trumps one hundred degrees. After the court case was settled and the sentence was given, my father hired Willie after hours to help him make his kitchen cabinets.

Now, if my father was able, you can be sure he would have built the cabinets himself. He and Babette did all of the demolition. They replastered difficult arches. Knocked down walls. Replaced hardwood. Moved the plumbing. The electrical. Designed the entire remodel. But my father had begun to see real signs of his disease, and month after month he became able to do less and less.

Willie was an amazing woodworker. He, like many laborers in El Paso, had done and could do a little bit of everything. He'd laid asphalt, brick, tile, done plumbing, welded. But also like many laborers he remains, and probably always will be, a laborer. I just don't know what it takes for a smart kid like Willie, who speaks three languages including sign language (the mother of Willie's daughter was deaf), is highly skilled, and has street smarts to boot, to go from the laborer to the employer. Or why some people manage to get out of a bad situation, but most probably don't. It's easy over a glass of wine with your lucky friends to talk about how everyone in America has opportunity and all they really need to do is seize it, but my best guess is if your uncle shot you in the face when you were twelve, you're really just trying to seize not getting shot in the face again.

Willie helped my dad and Babette build a stellar kitchen, and he helped on occasion when my dad fell, or when someone needed to watch him while Babette ran an errand. He'd been coming on and off to our house working on miscellaneous projects for the better part of five years. They finished the kitchen cabinets about a year after they started and right before Willie went to prison for almost two.

The Tax Assessor's office calls to let us know that VIN Inspections would be coming by our house. VIN inspections, I learn, was typically out looking for stolen cars. The VIN (Vehicle Identification Number) is how they identify a car uniquely. If someone steals a car, for example, and paints it a different color, the VIN is stamped all over it (on the engine, the frame) and it can be easily identified by that number. That's what they were doing for untitled vehicles. They find the VIN, look it up, and make sure it's actually yours (or non-existent), and clear you to get a proper title.

"Coming by" turned out to be several weeks, but four officers in plain clothes eventually arrive at our house on a random weekday morning. I hurry to the back garage and try to clear a space for the officers to get a look at the car. There are no lights in the garage, and there isn't a clean way to walk around it. It's full of dust and junk. Willie, out of prison by this time and back working for my dad, shows the officers to the backyard.

I introduce myself and thank them for coming.

"Officer Olivas." The first man offers his hand to shake. "You got a great piece of property here."

"Thank you," I answer on behalf of my father. "Big yards down here in the valley." The Upper Valley with its big backyards and green trees fed by the Rio Grande sits on the west side of the Franklin Mountains. The Lower Valley, by contrast, sits on the southeast side, with some areas not even having potable water until recent decades.

I walk around the driver's side of the dusty car and show the officers the number that was stamped on the inside of the driver's door frame which I think might be the VIN number. "This is the only thing I've seen that looks like it might be a VIN," I say and point to the number.

Officer Olivas pulls out a flashlight and has a look. The other three officers climb around the car with flashlights and look for another number hiding somewhere.

"We might have to strip the paint to see it clearly," says Officer Olivas.

A fifth officer joins from the front yard to have a look. This guy looks like he could be a model. Tall. Good looking. Muscular. None of these guys look like cops. They just look like regular dudes and I'm guessing that was what they were supposed to look like when they weren't in uniform. Like regular dudes who just happen to be looking for stolen cars. I tell Officer Olivas the quick story about the '41. About my father. I ask him a couple cop questions.

The fifth officer pulls a laptop out of his bag and then with rubber gloves and a flashlight heads to the front of the car. The car is parked rear end out. Two officers remove the hood of the car, which is just resting on the body and not bolted to anything. They set it aside out on the grass. None of the officers pay any attention to the Colorado license plate that is on the front of the car from 1972. Eddie Solis told me after this long, that didn't really matter anymore anyway.

The officers spend a bit of time looking around the body. They write a few things down and come back outside. Officer Olivas tells me that the best next step for me is to turn the car around in the garage so that they can jack it up in the front and get underneath. The car can't be jacked up in the garage since there is no more room left from the back wall to the front of the car, so that means I need to inflate the tires and push the car out of the garage, turn it around, and then push it back into the garage.

It will be four months before I turn the '41 around.

I start brushing my father's teeth. That's how we mark negative progress. By the things that my father becomes unable to do. When I got home to El Paso I could place his toothbrush in his hands and like the computer mouse he could hold his left hand with his right hand and put it in his mouth. We used to be able to do the same with a glass so he could rinse his mouth, but his hands had slowly weakened and were beginning to turn upwards with his fingers curling into frozen ALS fists. So now we lean his wheelchair back like a dentist's chair and brush his teeth for him, but not too far so he doesn't choke on the toothpaste. Then we raise it to counter height so that he can spit in the sink and then we hold a glass to his mouth to rinse. There is always food in his teeth, on his tongue, and around his gums. He takes pills that reduce the amount of saliva in his mouth so he won't choke while swallowing which means there is nothing to wash it down anymore. You don't really think about the simple regular cleaning your body does to itself, like wash your mouth out.

You can also hear the progress starting in my father's voice. There are slurs. He talks a little slower. His voice is quieter as it becomes harder for his lungs to push air over his vocal chords. Some days are worse than others. And then on a random day he'll talk normally and you think maybe you imagined it. Then ALS would remind you that you hadn't.

One day my father asks to use his breathing machine while he takes a nap. Like many ALS patients do as their breathing deteriorates, my father uses a BIPAP to help him breathe during the night. A BIPAP is like one of those fighter-pilot-looking mask things that people wear to stop snoring, except a BIPAP pushes more air into your lungs if you aren't doing it yourself. Some doctors call it a non-invasive tracheotomy tube. Instead of a tube in your throat, it pushes air through your nose and mouth and into your lungs so you don't have to work as hard to breathe. Since respiratory failure is the cause of death for so many ALS victims, difficulty breathing is a bad thing. On occasion we bring the machine by his computer if he feels like he needs it.

As I lie on the couch one afternoon, my father pulls up next to me in his chair. He asks me to put my feet up on his legs and he uses one hand to slowly lift the other hand and tries to use his soft knuckles to rub my feet.

Our collie Missy dies on a Sunday morning while my father and I are eating breakfast at my aunt and uncle's, and Babette is at a farmers market on the other side of town. I think my dad and I both had a feeling she might go that morning and that maybe we should have stayed with her, but neither of us said anything to each other about it and we went anyway. We eat pancakes. My dad has but a few bites and is quiet, like he seems to be more often these days.

When my sister and I were toddlers we had our picture on the front page of the El Paso Times sitting in the middle of a litter of poodles in our backyard. We'd always had poodles. There was Trey and Licorice, Tarbaby (it was the seventies), Houston, Nigel, and now Krinkle. After Nigel died, my father started getting rescue dogs at the pound. Maggie was the fattest lab you'd ever seen. Little Fella, once actually a little fella, had grown to a pony-like German Shepherd of one hundred sixty pounds. And then there was Missy.

Missy lay in the same position on the cool terra cotta tile for three days, unable to move due to some disease I can't pronounce and am not really sure she had in the first place. She wouldn't take her medicine, wouldn't eat, and finally wouldn't drink.

She wheezed and coughed. She spit up bile. Her breathing kept me awake even upstairs. I came down to pet her during each night as she got worse. I carried her outside to lie in the late night breeze. Krinkle and Little Fella came with me and we listened to the trees. Little Fella kept watch by her all night not anywhere near where he usually slept.

Before we left for breakfast my father pulls up next to her. I raise the arm of his chair and lean him off of the side, just low enough so that he can touch Missy and tell her he loves her.

I know Missy is gone when I turn the corner, and I tell my father before he makes it into the hallway.

My father sobs for his dog. He sobs that we should have stayed. That she died alone. That dogs take nothing. That she was the sweetest dog he ever had. He asks me to put a blanket over her body. I say I'm so sorry and that maybe we should have stayed. But that maybe she waited until we were all gone. Maybe she wanted to die alone. I don't know.

Babette comes home shortly after we do.

She holds my father in his wheelchair and they cry together.

Babette agrees that maybe Missy didn't want us to be there when she passed. That she waited until we left. When she was alone with her brother and sister dogs.

She calls a vet that's open on a Sunday. I pick Missy's stiff heavy body up and carry her to our Suburban. We drive to the other side of town near the airport and wait in the parking lot. I carry Missy to my father in the passenger seat. Babette pulls her blanket back and my father reaches to her. He pets her wiry coat with the back of his hand and his curled up fingers. He says goodbye to Missy in a blubbering ALS slur.

The summer passes quietly and gives into the fall. On a September Saturday morning we drive to Albuquerque, New Mexico for the annual New Mexico Walk for ALS, which raises money for the state ALS Association, along with my aunt and uncle, my step-uncle and his wife, and the rest of our team, the Southwest Mountain Movers. The walk is the following Sunday morning. We raised seventeen thousand dollars as a team. The most by any team at the walk.

I sit in my hotel room. My father is sleeping in the adjoining room while everyone else is out shopping. My uncle says that he thought he just didn't want to face the day, which may have been the case as our ride up wasn't the greatest. My father sat sadly in the passenger seat. His head seemed to be hanging lower as if he was losing the muscles that kept it upright. His butt was burning, he explained, from sitting in one position for hours upon hours. As we drove, his body would slowly slide down the seat under the seatbelt and press up against the dash until the pain against his bony knees was too much and the seat belt had moved all the way up to his chin and we would pull over and readjust him. We had replaced the passenger seat with a special seat with a lift that turned it out of the car and lowered it down to the ground. When we'd stop I'd turn and lower him out into the fresh air.

The drive to Albuquerque is a beautiful one north up I-25 following the Rio Grande. Anything near the river is green straddled by brown and red. The river is an oasis of sorts in the desert. As you get closer to Albuquerque the terrain turns a darker green on its way to northern New Mexico and Colorado.

My father and I watch the Texas game in the hotel room and I guess that he secretly wants them to lose since I think he still wished all his children had gone to Texas A&M, born somewhere out of the Texas Sigma Alpha Epsilon fraternity's disapproval of his facial hair at a party once in Austin. Like he wished we were all doctors and played the violin, but really I think my dad wished he went to A&M, was a doctor, and played the violin, heartbreakingly described by him being so terrified of his music teacher in grade school that when she asked young Blu Jr. what instrument he wanted to play he just flailed his arms around and she gave him a trombone.

Sunday morning is the ALS walk at the minor league baseball stadium, Isotopes Park, where four hundred walkers are split up into teams with shirts decorated with team names like "Team Sanchez" or "Renie's Roadrunners" and we walk three miles around the upper deck. Getting together with other ALS sufferers, called PALS (Person with ALS), and caregivers is supportive in some ways, and just plain sad in so many others. Everyone wanders around and talks to each other. You give the sufferers a once over and try to gauge how bad their progression is. How long they have. How old they are.

Raising money to support the PALS is critical. It's estimated that the average cost of caring for an ALS patient in the latter years of the disease approaches two hundred thousand dollars a year. My father recently showed me an email from a PAL asking for donations so he didn't lose his house. We would send him a hundred dollars in the morning.

My dad wheels over to the memorial wall where there are photos of those who have died from ALS. That's the saddest part. We stand in silence and look at the photos. Calculate the dates. Determine who was the youngest. How good they looked healthy, and how fast the disease took them. There are two on the wall from our group.

We take a team photo. We are glad to be there and I'm glad some of our family made the trip. We walk together to raise money, and "because we can" says our motto, and because what the fuck else can we do?

My father stops after one lap. It's too hot and his head is hanging down. We get an orange and some water and watch the men's softball game on the field.

Maybe the most torturous part of living with ALS, if you can actually call one thing *the* most torturous thing out of a long list of pretty darn torturous things, has to be the itching, or rather, the inability to scratch an itch. If you consider it, you'll see that you scratch your nose, or your head, or your arm, or your whatever fifty or a hundred or even more times a day. You never think about it. If you have an itch, you just scratch it. You brush over your nose like it's no big deal. Scratch your arm. Your head. You probably don't even realize you itched at all. It's just one of those normal things you do because you have arms and hands that work the way they're supposed to work when your brain tells them to work that way. But as my father loses the ability to lift his arms and then to use his hands it has become virtually impossible for him to scratch himself.

"Blu."

"Yes."

"Nose."

I get up and scratch his nose.

I sit down.

"Blu."

"Yes!"

"Right side." Because itches always seemed to travel. Like one side is jealous of the other.

I get up and scratch the right side of his face.

I sit down.

"Blu."

"Yes!!"

"Head."

And it goes on like this pretty much all day long, every single day. In the morning. During the day. At night. In bed.

Picture me in the living room with both hands wrapped around a wooden back scratcher while I claw my father's crotch like I'm a digging a ditch.

"GOOD GOD!" He yells in fucking euphoria. My poor father can't even scratch his own balls.

I drive my father to the El Paso Veterans Administration for a dentist appointment. The VA is located on the Ft. Bliss Army Base. Ft. Bliss, home of the Patriot Missile, is on the northeast side of El Paso directly over the Franklins. The Patriot Missile was the weapon of glory in the first Gulf War, most famous for destroying Saddam Hussein's SCUD missiles on the fly. El Paso has rallied around the Patriot. There is a Patriot Elementary School, Patriot Car Sales, Patriot Apartments. Even the freeway to Ft. Bliss is named the Patriot Freeway. But if you aren't in the Army, a vet, work on the base, or just don't live on the northeast side of town, you don't see too much of Ft. Bliss.

My father is a veteran. But he's never been a flag-waving veteran. He's never worn a Navy hat. He's never had any bumper stickers on his cars. He is mostly unassuming, but make no mistake, he loves the military. It's all we watch on TV. 287. That's the military channel. When we turn on the TV, 287. If you want to watch Fringe? 287. The news? 287. If all else fails? 287. His military and weapons knowledge is impressive.

My father served in the Navy for only two short years during the Vietnam conflict. He was aboard the U.S.S. Cannisteo, which, for his fortunate sake, ended up under repair during the time he and the ship were scheduled to depart. He made training trips to Cuba and talked about one to the Mediterranean but no trips for combat.

The VA considers Lou Gehrig's Disease a one hundred percent covered service-related disease. That is, your disability is completely covered financially. The statistics say you're twice as likely to get ALS as a veteran. There are theories about military vaccinations, chemical weapons, or other toxins, but the truth still remains that no one actually knows why the statistics are so high.

Almost all of my father's doctor's appointments are now at the VA. The eye doctor, the dentist, the urologist. Without question, if I had a choice, which of course I do not as a regular citizen, I would go to the VA a thousand times before I'd set foot in another private doctor's office. Before my dad got sick I had never been to a VA. I had no real reason to, of course, but I had heard enough horror stories from the news and such to feel pretty good about my over-priced health insurance, my occasional trips to the doctor, my growing fear of medical care, and the hell I go through every time I have to have a conversation with my insurance company, like that one time when I went in for a routine physical and the doctor submitted a claim to my insurance for something along the lines of "high blood pressure relating to deviant sexual behavior" and it took me over two years to get it sorted out. No I will not read my health handbook thank you very much, but if you would like, you can take your private health insurance and deviantly stick it up your ass.

You can feel the brotherhood at the VA. There are people old and young. Male and female. Many people wear their war hats. Vietnam. Gulf War. A rare World War II. They talk to each other in the waiting rooms. There's just a feeling of something in common that's hard to describe. It's something that I don't have, nor ever will, and am envious of.

People look at me and nod. They smile. They bless me. They know that many vets are not taken care of, and they thank me silently every time I walk through the hospital behind my father's wheelchair. I don't want the thanks, because I don't feel like I deserve any thanks, but I appreciate it for my father.

As we leave the VA that day, we run right into the man who some thirty-odd years earlier repainted the '41. My father hasn't seen him since. He, like many people these days, doesn't recognize my dad. We chat a bit about the car and my father. We exchange numbers. He reaches down and squeezes my father's hand.

The people closest to the PALS get it the worst. The caregivers. That's what we're told anyway. That the patients have lost complete control of their world and the only thing they have any control of at all is their anger. They will lash out. Put you down. Say cruel things. They will even sometimes try to hurt you physically. And you will react in ways you would never dream of reacting. You'll take it personally. You'll scream. Lash out. Put them down. Say cruel things. But I've sort of dismissed this, as I suspect many caregivers do, as something that would probably not happen to my father and me, or wasn't happening to my father and me.

But the fighting has started and it's getting worse.

We fight about the most ridiculous things—a parking space, the way I eat my cereal, the GPS. But it's as if we're fighting about something like me finally having the courage to confront him for years of childhood abuse (which of course there was none).

I ask my dad at Costco why he needs a third GPS. But not like, "What kind of fool wants a third GPS?" More like, or at least what I thought was more like, I just ask in the midst of conversation at the Costco since, you know, he already had two GPSs.

"Because I fucking want a third GPS!" he screams back at me.

Which leads to a nasty exchange by the electronics section, him asking for the money back that he lent me in college to make my first crappy album, and me storming off to the men's clothing (and then back again because Babette was somewhere else in the store).

Or the time my dad asked me to go to Home Depot to buy a trowel. We have buckets of trowels in the garage so I asked him, "Do you want a flat trowel or a foam trowel?" thinking surely we had whatever he needed in the garage somewhere.

And he snapped, "Did I say I wanted a fucking foam trowel?"

To which I responded by throwing the trowel against the wall and stomping up to my bedroom.

Sometimes after an argument he'll drive back into his bedroom and just sit in his wheelchair as far away from me as he can get and it feels like he's miles away.

We waste an incredible amount of energy on worthless arguments. My father doesn't hate me for asking about a trowel. My guess is what he really hates is the fact that he can't pick up a trowel, turn it on its side, grab the handle, hold it up to the brick, point to it, move it, and *teach* me about the trowel. But he can't teach me. He can only be angry. That's all he can do.

I've always gotten along with my father. I was a young athlete. He was my coach. He was a lawyer. I was his loud-mouthed son. Like it was supposed to be, or usually was, I thought. When my mother left twenty-five years ago I was thirteen. She took my sister and my younger brother back to Ohio with her to be closer to her family. I stayed in El Paso with my father. He worked. I was home alone. But home was an easy walk from school. I often walked with my buddy Chuck Crowder.

The Crowders owned the Santa Teresa Country Club, not too far up the street from our house in Santa Teresa, New Mexico. Mr. Crowder bought land in the middle of absolutely nowhere and along with Lee Trevino, the professional golfer, built an amazing country club and residential development, which now many years later has an airport, a high school, and even a border crossing into Mexico. Mr. Crowder was the quintessential Texas cowboy, complete with a suit, a giant cowboy hat, snake skin boots, a pocket watch, and stories that couldn't possibly be true but probably were.

Mr. Crowder shrewdly bought the water rights to the property under Santa Teresa when he first purchased the land many years ago. Thirty years later as El Paso struggled to keep enough water in their own city, the water rights became nearly invaluable. And as money tends to do, it brought the sharks.

City governments in Texas and New Mexico wanted to just annex the water. Every dirt bag politician within ear shot wanted the water. And every businessman in the southwest would stop at essentially nothing to get what was about next to owning air.

Once during high school, Chuck wouldn't leave his house sometimes for fear of being kidnapped.

After years of exhaustive battling and spending every last dime, the Crowders eventually sold everything, including the water rights, and moved from what was one of the nicest homes I've ever set foot in, to an unassuming two bedroom apartment. Mr. and Mrs. Crowder divorced.

Somewhere along the line the mix of money, pressure, and subsequent failure after failure was too much for Chuck to handle. He developed a pill problem which led to a drinking problem or vice versa.

The last time I saw Chuck was while I was living in New York City. He showed up one night at my girlfriend's apartment after sleeping in a city park the night before. I let him in and we had a fairly sobering, no pun intended, conversation about being fucked up. About hitting rock bottom. About making a fresh start. He got a beer out of the fridge because, "You can't just quit cold turkey." We talked about him coming out on the road with me just to get away. I said he was welcome any time. The motels and gas were paid for. I took a cab with him to Penn Station. I bought him a train ticket to DC where we had a couple old El Paso friends and that seemed like a better place for him to stay. I gave him the last twenty dollars in my wallet. We took a phone picture together. I kissed him on the cheek and told him I loved him.

Two weeks later he walked into his garage and put a shotgun to his chest.

It's hard to quantify how exactly my father is declining and how fast. You just kinda know one day. Occasionally it's obvious. On one morning he wet the bed because we didn't get to him fast enough. It's hard to think of anything more humiliating than being a sixty-eight-year-old man who wets his bed, and worse than that, a man who can't move and has to lie in his own urine. We change his clothes like we change my little two-year-old niece Emory's clothes after she wets her diaper.

It becomes exhausting. Because he isn't breathing right he gets scared and doesn't want to go to sleep. And even after he does, he calls out during the night and I have to get him up out of bed and sit him on the edge of his mattress, which seems to help a little. He sits there until he's so painfully tired that he has no choice but to sleep. That might happen at midnight. Then he does it again at four thirty. Then maybe at six thirty. Maybe we watch TV and if he's lucky he falls back asleep again when there's daylight.

Before he'll even think about sleep now, he makes me show him the baby monitor in my hand so he knows I can hear him.

I move downstairs for good, back into my old bedroom, so I can be closer to my father during the night and I sleep with the door open. The entire upstairs becomes a closet he will never see again.

Eight months gone. I acknowledge it to myself mostly because I can't believe I've been home for eight months, and partly because in eight months I've done effectively nothing with the '41. In two hundred and forty days I've been waiting for people to call me back, for things to go the way everyone told me they were supposed to go, and maybe for them to just happen, but no one really calls and nothing goes the way it's supposed to, and no one is really gonna do anything for me. It's almost Christmas and I have no title to the car and have done a sum total of absolutely nothing to it.

Every day I write a to do list on a three by five index card and put it on my desk. Air compressor oil, air compressor plug, frame, print photos, magnetic tape, 41. Every day I put "41" on the list. And every day it goes un-done. Then I write it again on a clean card the next day. And the next. And then the next.

But with my father getting worse, and the title feeling like a bit of a lost cause, I decide waiting is just something I can't do anymore. I decide to change direction, start work on the '41, and tackle the title somewhere down the road. At this point, it doesn't seem like there is really any other choice.

I fly to San Antonio a few days before Christmas to see my mother who has flown in for the holidays to stay with my sister. I haven't seen her at all this year; not unlike my younger years when she was so far away in Ohio. My uncle stays over to help. Our neighbor Doug comes by when they need to move my father. My cousin comes over in the mornings to help get his uncle out of bed and then to hold him up with his pants around his ankles while Babette wipes him after he takes a shit on a plastic toilet in the kitchen. A plastic toilet in the wide open kitchen proves to be sometimes easier than the real toilet even in the big bathroom, we find, and especially in a hurry.

I call my father on Skype one afternoon with my niece. Babette answers. My dad is front and center. I sit next to my niece and my sister, pregnant with her next baby girl.

"Where Gampa?" Emory asks.

And there he is. But I'm looking at a different man. My father in skin and bones. Like the skeleton trees, I wrote in a poem.

the skeleton trees

the leaves fell

and the colors went away

we sat next to the fire

as the wind blew

my father nearly bones

like the skeleton trees

His frail arms against his sides. His curled hands in his lap. His head cocked far to the left and down slightly because he can control it less and less and his big heavy head just goes that way. A pillow around his neck. A blanket over his legs.

My mother said she hardly recognized him in the Christmas card they sent my sister this year. I always wondered how in the world that could really be. My father had changed but not so much that he looked unrecognizable, to me anyway. And then today in some ways I feel like I barely know the man on the screen. He looks so small. So weak. Like he's dying. My mother says he used to be so strong and God bless him. I want to go home.

Little Emory steals the show. Crazily waving with two year old vigor. Pointing at "the doggie!" Putting stickers on her belly. Putting stickers on my belly. Turing circles. Jumping up and down. My father laughs. It's good to see him laugh.

They're getting ready for their Christmas party. It's going to be a big Syrian bash. Had she been alive, Babette's mother would have made all the food. It's what I remember most about her family. The food. Arab women cook all damn day.

I come home to an older, thinner, weaker man. It's as if my father has aged in just the week that I was gone. His voice is softer. He's more vulnerable. Less able.

My plane is two hours late. It's snowing in El Paso with fifty mile per hour winds. I walk in the door and straight to my father. I kiss him several times, hug his bones, and we immediately take a shit in the plastic toilet in the kitchen.

It has rapidly gotten to the point where my father can do effectively nothing on his own. When I got home last May, he could just about hold a glass in his hands and sip a drink through a straw. Now he can't hold a glass at all. He could move a mouse on the computer. Now he can't lift his arm high enough to get it anywhere near the mouse. But he could wheel himself to the desk at least. More and more he asks me to control his chair because he is slowly losing his ability to do that too.

Days are just like other days. Nights grow worse. He's like a boulder now. His neck muscles are stiff and painful from being all but frozen. His arms ache. His hips hurt. Each morning, no matter what the weather, we put a pair of gray warmup shorts around his knees while he sits on the edge of the bed. Babette warms up his shirts in the microwave because all of a sudden he seems to be cold all the time and it's just too difficult to put pants or a jacket on him. Every day, all day, no matter where we go, it's gray warmup shorts and a short sleeve collared shirt. The gray shorts because for some reason gray warmup shorts are more flexible than other colors, and warmup because we can more easily move them over and give him a urinal. No zippers. No pulling pants down. And a shirt with a collar because they're easier to get around his head and the short sleeves because long sleeves are a hassle.

I wrap my body around his body. I struggle to lift him but then stand up with him and pause, and either Babette or I reach and pull his shorts up. Then I twist and dump his lump of a body into his chair. Then I grab him under his shoulders and in one motion lift him up and simultaneously push my knee against his knee which helps push him back and up and all the way into his chair. He slides down and I do it again, all day long. One of us makes him coffee. He can still drink coffee.

John Attel calls to tell me his friend George McCool is taking a 250 straight six out of his Chevelle and that it runs good and I should buy it from him. I call and we exchange messages. We wish each other a happy holiday and say we'll get back in touch after the new year.

My dad and I sit in the garage and talk about where in the world I am gonna work on the car. It isn't realistic to work on it in the back garage. It's too full of junk and there's no electricity and no tools.

We have a giant tent over our carport in front of our proper garage which would be ideal to work under, but for the last couple years has also held a twenty-five-foot trailer underneath it which has been the staging area for various house projects. Sheets of plywood are stacked on it next to twenty-foot lengths of angle steel. Even all my Rubbermaid tubs of junk I brought home from Nashville still sit on top of it. Carlos used the steel to build various things like a new base for the table saw, a welding table, a large work bench and some furniture for my brother. I suggest I could put the wood and steel in the backyard and swap the trailer for the '41. Or another possibility was to clean out our actual garage and work on the '41 inside the garage. Part of that wood that was sitting on the trailer has been used to finally, after decades, actually organize the garage. There were now custom cabinets with HDPE counter tops (High Density Polyurethane, the material out of which they make cutting boards). Each major tool has its own rolling cabinet with an HDPE top. The miter saw. The joiner. The sander. The planer. The dovetailer. Then there are seven-foot rolling cabinets with drawers to hold every single miscellaneous thing in the garage. And there are two seven-foot expandable cabinets that open up to hang levels, hammers, squares and such. There's a high end table saw, a vacuum to suck up the sawdust, a mig welder, a plasma cutter, a giant compressor. My dad's addiction.

"Just make a decision," he says to me softly.

"Ok," I tell him. "Then I'm gonna move the wood and put the trailer in the backyard and then maybe Carlos and I can push the car around."

"What about the trailer when we irrigate in the spring?"

"I'll deal with that in the spring."

In the lobby of the eye doctor my father informs me that he "may need to sit down," which is code for needing to use the restroom, but my father would never say he *needed* to sit down, or he needed to do anything really. If you could, or if it's not too much trouble, were a close second and third. It's his subtle way of saying "I don't wanna be a burden," whenever he needs you for something. It's the exact opposite of the anger. It's deliberate and controlled. He hates that people have to do things for him. The anger comes and goes. It's a manifestation of the situation, whereas to him the burden never leaves.

"Tell me what you want, Dad. Don't say may. Say what you need. You don't need to be polite to me."

We wheel into a handicap stall. I put my hands under his shoulders and pull him out on the seat to where his feet touch the ground and his body is almost falling off the chair. I take one step back and pull his body towards mine, his legs collapse, and we fall in a heap onto the sticky urine-coated men's room floor.

My father cries out in pain. "MY LEGS!! MY LEGS!!" He may actually be crying. Just bending his legs is like someone pulling them off of him.

I panic. He panics. We panic. I try to lift him but he's just dead weight. I try again. I use my legs. We slide around in several people's dripped piss. I manage to get him sort of sitting upright. We fall again.

"MY LEGS!"

"I'm trying to help you!"

"MY LEGS!"

"I'M TRYING TO HELP YOU!" I scream and put my back up against the wall and manage to wiggle us up into a standing position. I hold him up against the chair with my right arm and with my left arm turn the chair on and lower it to where I can put him on the seat. His legs are collapsing again, but the seat is low enough to get him onto the edge. I stand and grab my throbbing lower back.

My defeated father sits on the edge of the chair. His gut hangs out of his shirt.

Someone knocks on the stall door. We decide not to take a shit.

My father can't sleep. His right knee is swollen. His right hip is throbbing. He sleeps on his left side but the pressure causes that side of his body to hurt and we change to the right. I convince him to lie on his back and tilt the bed up, but I turn him back on his side in the middle of the night. ALS is not a painful disease, but ALS is a painful disease.

I crush up ibuprofen and put it in his tube. We start to give him medicine through his feeding tube because pills are becoming too hard to swallow. Each morning we grind up twenty-some-odd pills that do who knows what (really nobody seems to know), and dissolve them in water with a mortar and pestle. Then we suck the vomit-green liquid into a giant syringe and push the mixture into his feeding tube. Then we repeat each night.

I rub my father's throbbing knees. I tell him I don't know what to do.

"Nothing is going right," he tells me.

I rub his knees again, "I know."

"What exactly do I need to get an engine from a truck to the '41?" I ask John Attel.

"Tequila and bandages."

2011 arrives and I drive the forty miles to Horizon City to buy the 250 engine. Horizon City was at one time what it sounded like. Way out on the horizon. But what used to be the horizon is now just east El Paso. There is a Best Buy. A Starbucks. A PetSmart. Just like any other homogenized American city.

I meet George McCool at a scrappy cinderblock car shop behind a car wash on an empty side of town. There are cars, parts, old tires, piles of things, a cliché barking dog on a rope eating bites from a mound of dog food placed on the ground beneath him. There are a few men huddled in a group at the car wash doing who knows what.

George meets my truck at the gate. We shake hands and introduce ourselves through the driver's window. The shop owner follows behind him.

"Hola. Mucho gusto." I give my standard Spanish intro. *Hi. Nice to meet you.*

George points towards the fence to an engine dangling on a cherry picker. The cherry picker, a small crane made to pick up a heavy engine, uses the same principal as the lift we have at home that, should we need it, picks my father up out of bed or off of the floor.

I park and we walk over to the engine and he says, "It's got the starter, the carburetor…" the something and the something else. "It's all there." None of that, of course, meaning much of anything to me.

I back my truck into the shop yard and up to the cherry picker. The shop owner guides me in. He grabs an old tire from a stack of old used tires and throws it in my truck bed. He and George slowly push and bump the cherry picker under the truck, guide the heavy engine block into the truck bed, and carefully lower it into the tire like a cradle. The shop owner puts another tire under the top-heavy side of the engine so it won't roll. George puts the shifter in the bed before I drive off without it, and I put the air filter in my back seat so it won't fly out on the way home. It's a manual transmission, but easy to make an automatic, John Attel had said.

I look at the engine. It's big. It's heavy. There are wires everywhere and lots of grease. I give George four hundred dollars, we shake hands again, and I drive away.

I stop by a Harbor Freight on the way home to get a cherry picker of my own so that I can get the engine back out of the truck. My father is like a kid in a candy store in Harbor Freight. He absolutely loves the place. Harbor Freight is the Dollar Store for tools. They have just about every tool you've ever wanted and then like a thousand other tools and they're all cheaper than anywhere else. They're physically small stores and have somehow carved a niche in a market dominated by Home Depot and Lowe's. They sell cheap Chinese tools and give them American sounding names like "Chicago" and "US General." I find an elusive employee and after paying we load a two-ton engine jack next to the engine in my truck.

My father is sleeping in his wheelchair wrapped like a mummy in two blankets when I get home because no one can quite get him in bed as smoothly as I can. His old friend Vince from high school kept an eye on him while I drove to get the engine. Vince is tall and bald and still has the frame of a once-ruthless high school football player but is now just a tall, bald, warm-hearted story teller.

"Your father is my only true friend," he once told me.

On his way out Vince has a look at the engine. He says he'll come back by later to help me get it out of the truck.

"I can do it," I assure him.

"No," he says with a bit of a smile. "No you can't."

And Vince was right.

I sit with my dad until he wakes up and then we go out to the truck to look at the engine.

He glances it over from his chair.

"Does it look right?" I ask him.

"Oh yeah," he says to my relief, because frankly if I saw this greased up old block sitting on the ground and someone asked me if it was any good, I'd probably have just said throw it in the garbage because I have no real clue if an engine is any good unless it's in a car and I'm driving.

The cherry picker is in two heavy boxes. I slide them out of the bed, put them both on a floor dolly, and wheel them in the gate and in front of the trailer.

I open the boxes and pull out a notoriously awful Harbor Freight instruction manual complete with the most ridiculously detailed and unintuitive line drawings. Dotted lines from a sketch of a bolt to the hole where you put it, if you can actually follow the lines, and what might as well be an optical illusion of the bolt hovering in thin air. Is it on the top or is it on the bottom? I'm looking for an M18 bolt which is, I thought, 3 5/16 inches long. No idea what an M18, M16, M14 or M anything else is. No bolt measures 3 5/16 or any other measurement that the manual says. I lose my patience. I curse the Chinese. I throw a couple things.

After a bit more cussing and a little more reading I manage to start assembling what is really a pretty simple piece of equipment. I make another three or four trips to the garage to get various socket sizes and about an hour later I have myself a bright orange, brand spanking new cherry picker. I'm proud of myself even though it was technically about as easy as putting together an Ikea shelf.

Doug peeks over from his yard and comes over for a look. There was a time when my father and Doug almost came to blows over probably something stupid like who knew more about sprinkler systems or something, but that time has thankfully passed and Doug and his wife CJ are just our neighbors now. They feed our dogs when we're away. They come over for dinner. They walk with Babette and Krinkle every morning. And most importantly these days, Babette calls Doug if I'm not around and my father has fallen or she can't get him onto the toilet or something that requires a little more strength than she has.

Doug knows a lot about a lotta things just like my dad does. I show him the engine and tell him it's for the '41 in the back.

"That's a late model engine for a '41," he says.

"I think it's late sixties," I say not really knowing but vaguely remembering John Attel mentioning it.

He wastes no time and hops up into the truck bed and starts looking around for bolts on the engine where we can hook the picker. I grab a chain from the garage. I show him where George McCool put the chain and suggest we wrap the chain around whatever the thing was that I was pointing at. Doug puts the chain about where he thinks is best for balance, threads the chain through the hook on the lift, and I pump the lift like a tire jack. After a few pumps the engine slowly lifts up and off the tire in which it had been resting. The tire starts to slide towards the tailgate as it raises because of the weight, and the lift starts to move towards the engine and pushes the tailgate shut. I lower the engine and Doug readjusts the chain to take out a little slack. The second time is a charm and the engine smoothly and quite easily lifts up and out of the tire, and we slowly push the lift away from the truck bed and in the direction of the trailer. I put down some oil absorbent carpet that my dad has lying around. Doug grabs the tire from the truck bed and puts it on the trailer and I lower the engine with a hiss into the tire once again, just low enough to take the strain off the chain.

I shake Doug's hand and he heads on back to his house.

"That's the easy part," he calls over his shoulder.

"I was afraid of that!"

My very own engine is now resting peacefully on the trailer under the carport tent. I take a picture with my phone and send it to my brother and wish he was there to work on it with me. I wheel my father into the house.

Going on nine months and this is my first day of actual progress. It feels good.

More days pass and my father has more trouble breathing. We're up all night. And another night. And another. Babette stands at the bed. I lie on the floor while my dad sits on the edge of the bed. We wrap a blanket around his shoulders.

"Do you wanna raise the bed and lay on your back?"

"I don't know."

"Ok."

My sister and her daughter, my niece Emory, surprise my dad for a weekend visit.

"Where Gampa?" Emory asks as she walks in the door.

"Grandpa's sleeping," I tell her.

"Oh Ok. Kinkle!" She chases the poodle and Krinkle runs away.

We spend the weekend mostly at home. We laugh at Emory. We talk about my pregnant sister's next baby, Hannah. My sister confirms with me that it's ok to name her Hannah, as Hannah was my serious live-in girlfriend when I lived in New York City. I say well of course you can name her Hannah. I think about Hannah for the first time in a long time.

I take photographs of Emory running around the yard and then of my twin sister. She's beautiful and photogenic. I wonder to myself if I'll ever take photos of my child or my wife.

I text John Attel and ask what in the heck I'm supposed to do next. That evening he texts, "Are you home?" and drives up a minute later.

"Where's the car?" he asks.

"In the back," I say and point over the house.

We walk around the house to the backyard, into the back garage, and over to the '41. He does a once over, pokes around a bit, and tells me I need to take off the nose cone. Not really knowing what a nose cone is I ask, "All of this?" and motion to the front of the car.

"All of it. The fenders. The sides. All of it."

"Just up to the windshield?"

"Yep. You gonna work on it out here?"

"Probably under the tent on the carport."

"Good. 'Cause no one will hear you scream when something falls on you out here. And you need to decide if you want to go automatic or keep it standard."

"If I have a choice I guess I'd rather not shift."

He agrees and tells me I need to get a Powerglide. I have no idea, of course, what a Powerglide is. He explains that I have to take off the big silver thing (which is the manual transmission) that's attached to the engine, and replace it with another big silver thing that's a Powerglide. I know what the big silver thing is, but I still don't know what a Powerglide is or how it works or if it even glides.

We retreat inside the house and another long time neighbor, Don Cannon, is over to check on my dad. "Blu Boy!" He greets me each time I see him with his unique handshake, a little shaky these days from M.S.. His gray and yellow mustache from a lifetime of cigarettes makes me feel at home. Like I'm on my street. Like I never left.

"Uncle Bluie!" John says to my father, "We're gonna teach Junior what we did when we were kids!" and everybody laughs like they know something I don't. "Take a look at your knuckles," he instructs me and I look at my hands. "Remember what they look like because they won't look like that again."

Carlos drops by looking for work and after telling him we didn't have any asks if I can advance him a hundred dollars and he'll work it off the next time we need some work done. He needs it to pay rent. At least I think that's what he asks me in Spanish. Humiliating in any language, I gather.

Without hesitation my dad says, "Of course, lend him the money," and I feel guilty about feeling unsure in the first place. He comes back by in the afternoon and has a look at the roll-in bathroom door we decided needs to be moved a foot to the right so that my father's wheelchair doesn't need to make a turn to go through it and I choppily explain how I want to push the '41 around the house and put it in place of the trailer.

"Espero que el dinero ayuda," I tell him as he leaves. *I hope the money helps.*

"Bastante ayuda," he says. *It helps a lot.*

Carlos is at our house at eight the following morning and gets to work tearing down the door, while I start cleaning the trailer. There isn't too much left. The steel has been moved to the back garage. The wood sorted and organized. I take things one by one and put them on the ground by the sides of the trailer leaving enough room to pull the trailer out of the carport. I jack up the cherry picker and slowly move the heavy swinging engine back away from the trailer. Once I clear a path I whistle to Carlos.

"Listo?" He yells from the garage. *Ready?*

"Listo!" I call back to him and he stops the demolition and walks outside to help.

It's thirty degrees and windy. Winter has settled in.

I walk across the street to get our Suburban which we've parked at our feisty ninety-year-old neighbor Maggie Maguire's house because we have too many cars now in our driveway with mine and because Maggie likes to have cars parked at her house so she feels safer. She is the longest living neighbor on our street of ten houses at more than fifty years. Don around forty. My father just shy of that. Doug and CJ newer, but have clocked in more than twenty.

I back the Suburban into our driveway and throw the gate keys out the window to Carlos. He opens the gate and I back the hitch up to the trailer. Carlos locks the trailer into place and I do a once over to make sure nothing is hiding underneath. It's a long twenty-five foot trailer. As I pull out of the carport I look in the rearview at the space the trailer has occupied for the better part of four years. The concrete is a lighter shade of gray.

I take a right out of our driveway and into the street, then back up past the driveway, and pull up and over the lip of our front yard, around Babette's favorite palm tree, to where Carlos is now waiting by the gate on the other side of the house. He guides me through the gate and slowly, with a few starts and stops, along the house and into the backyard.

I had strung three long extension cords together and carried a small air compressor to the back garage the night before and aired up the tires on the '41. Three of the four still held decent air.

I open the creaky door and sit on the front seat in a puff of dust like I did as a kid, and Carlos, like an ox, gets behind the car. He pushes us out of the garage and down into the yard. I give the car a hard turn to the right and when we come to a stop, open the door and we push together. The car is light without an engine. We push it around the house and out into the street. It rolls easy on the asphalt.

Then we back it into Maggie Maguire's driveway and take a breath for the final push. It goes right up and into the driveway. Babette is sweeping the carport. My father is close to her in his wheelchair with blankets up to his neck to watch. I open the gate and we roll the '41 in. I get out of the car and put bricks around the tires so it won't move. I high five Carlos.

"No problemo," I say and he smiles.

"Claro que sí." *Agreed.*

I wonder to myself, if my father was able, how the day might have been different. Would we have pushed the '41 together around the house, out into the street, and into the carport, or would we have even done it at all.

I wheel him back into the house.

I park the Suburban back at Maggie's.

I cross the street and close the gate.

Eddie Solis calls to say he's bringing by some of the original '41 parts so that I can hang on to them, "for the purists." He pulls in the drive and I walk to meet him at his car. He has his buddy and right hand man Johnny with him. Johnny is an American but lives in Juarez, and given the state of Juarez these days, none of us can quite understand why.

Eddie opens his hatchback to a big cardboard box of old greasy car parts. He points out the transmission, which seems small compared to the one attached to my engine, the starter, and something else that looks like it could just as well be the starter. Everything looks like an antique. Brown. Dirty. Johnny helps me carry the parts in the gate. We put them on the planter and walk over to my new engine and Eddie and Johnny look it over.

I relay to Eddie that John Attel was over and recommended I get a Powerglide instead of using the manual transmission that was currently on the engine.

"You could do that," he says. "Or you could get a Turbo-Hydramatic 350."

"A what?"

"A TH350. A three speed. A Powerglide has two speeds. A 350 is three speeds and a 400 has four speeds."

"Says the guy who knows what he's talking about."

"Well, you're gonna learn!" he says. "You'll be much happier with a 350. More power."

"Now the other thing you're gonna need," Eddie tells me, "is an adapter kit to mount this engine and transmission onto the '41 frame."

"They make them for *that* engine to go on *this* car?"

"For just about every engine to every car. They sell them online. Easy to find."

We wander inside to say hi to my dad. Eddie sits on the big ten-by-ten rock fireplace my father built when he added on to the house.

Side note: Never ask your father if you can get rid of the extra fireplace rocks that have been sitting in a pile in the yard for thirty-five years if you don't know that there are fossils in the rocks that you've never paid attention to because you don't pay attention to anything.

I give Craigslist a shot later that evening just to see if by chance someone is selling a TH350 in the auto parts for sale section and find this listing:

> Dec 29 - Turbo 350 - $100 (Westside)
> TH350 - $100.00 OBO
> I was told that it was working when it was pulled from the car but cannot speak for it myself. Selling because I decided to go with a manual transmission.

A hundred bucks sounds cheap to me so I text, "Hi. Do you by chance still have the TH350?"

"Yes I do," a quick reply.

And since that was about the extent of the conversation I knew how to have with someone about a TH350, I call Eddie.

"Hey Eddie. I found a TH350 on Craigslist over here on the Westside for a hundred bucks. Does that sound good?"

"Does it have the torque converter?" he asks me.

"I have no idea."

"Does it have the torque converter?" I text back to the seller.

"Yes."

"Yes." (I've never even heard of a torque converter.)

I get the seller's address, Eddie comes by the next morning, and we drive together to look at the transmission.

It looks just like the manual transmission that's currently connected to my engine. Colin, a young skinny white kid who must be in high school, is standing in the garage and someone who looks like his mother is outside with him cleaning up the driveway.

Eddie walks around the transmission, gets up close and inspects it and offers sixty dollars for it which Colin accepts without a protest.

"Tip it so you don't let the torque converter fall out," Eddie instructs as Colin and I pick up the transmission and the torque converter slides out of it and slams onto the concrete.

"That," Eddie says.

Eddie sends an email in the morning pointing me to where I can buy the motor mounts and describing our next steps:

First, clean the TH350. I will bring you a can of cleaner to use. Don't roll it over on its side. Keep it as level as possible. Try and make the transmission look like new. Don't get water or grit, dirt or anything inside of it!

Second, we will re-seal it on the ground and out of the car.

Third, I will guide you through the removal of the standard transmission and flywheel from the engine.

Fourth, when we have the new flywheel for the TH350 we will reseal and attach it to the engine.

Having sat around for so long, we also need to look at the brakes because the rear end needs to be changed out.

I learn a few new things. Like that I have to change out the rear end and there's a flywheel on a transmission. Whatever that is.

My father sleeps through his BIPAP alarm. Technically the alarm is supposed to alert us that there's a problem with the machine, or that someone's stopped breathing or the mask isn't on correctly, but that's not really what it seems to ever mean with my father's machine, and the supremely irritating WHEEP! WHEEP! doesn't bother him in the least. It's like it isn't even happening. But one of us has to get up and walk to the bedroom and reset it every single time it goes off or it will just keep going off. That's a lot of trips to the bedroom, and it takes every shred of will not to smash it with a hammer to make it stop.

Controlling my anger is becoming more and more difficult. It seems to be a combination of things. The lack of sleep. The BIPAP alarm. The inability to do anything spontaneously. The whatever else it is.

We get in a blowout argument in the kitchen about stepping on my father's feet. His feet have become painfully sensitive as blood just pools in them and goes nowhere. Just a thump on his toes means searing pain. Some days they look like footballs. I can barely wash them in the shower it hurts him so badly. I lift him up to wash his face in the sink and he screams out (sometimes he summons the air to yell which is a surprise to us and probably even to himself) that I am carelessly stepping on his toes and refuse get off of them. Now I'm fairly certain I'm not just balancing on my father's toes. In my head I figure I may have stepped on them and moved my foot, but to him it feels like I'm just standing there on his feet. Rather than the obvious choice of maybe saying "I'm sorry, I didn't mean to step on your feet. Are you ok?" or a hundred other things I could say, I opt for something along the lines of, "I know when I'm standing on your goddamn feet and I WASN'T STANDING ON YOUR

GODDAMN FEET!" which in retrospect may have been an unwise choice.

I get angry. I storm off and pound on my computer keyboard checking my angry email. My father wheels out to the TV. Then he calls me to pick his nose and there is carrot cake on his TV stand so I pick his nose and feed him some carrot cake, and that's sometimes what it takes to put an argument behind us.

While my dad's taking a long nap in his chair I have time to sit and get to cleaning the transmission. I put my steel toes and my work jeans on and pull a stepstool from the garage next to the TH350. Eddie left a bag of his magical transmission elixir on the planter a few days back. I unbag it: a gas can of diesel fuel, kerosene, burnt motor oil, and a wire mechanic's brush.

"Brush it on the transmission but DO NOT get it in there," he had said and pointed to a hole in the transmission where the transmission fluid went, I presumed. "Let it sit for a day, preferably in the sun, and then wipe it off with a rag. Do it a second time but DO NOT get anything in there," he pointed to the hole again, "and just stay away from there too," he pointed to the back of the transmission, the side that connects to the engine. "Once you get it cleaned, call me and we'll go from there."

I put my dad's baby monitor on the hood of the '41, lay a sheet of the oil absorbent carpet on the ground, and roll the transmission over the carpet. Then I pick up the gas can and pour some of the black mixture into a used paint can I find on the side of the house. I grab the wire brush, dip it in the can, and start painting.

The transmission is dark and dirty. Covered in thick grease. Eddie said it looked like something had leaked from above it but not that the transmission itself had leaked. The grease is thinner on the top of the transmission and thicker where it had pooled below in the crevices. He also said it wasn't a bad looking tranny, though I can't tell the difference.

I paint his elixir all over the thing, carefully slowing down around the fluid hole and periodically poking a plastic sack back into it to protect it, careful not to spill anything into it. The transmission turns a wet greasy black, and after a few short minutes, when I brush over an area again, I can see the silver underneath peeking through.

I coat it top to bottom until it and my hands are covered in diesel and kerosene. It's getting dark so I call it a night.

I clean up and put my father in bed.

He grimaces as I delicately massage his once athletic legs.

He points them out. "Look at my legs," he says. "There's nothing there."

"I know. It's strange," I say and wrap my hands around them.

I sit next to his bed and rub them until he falls asleep.

My dad is constipated. But beyond any sort of constipation you've ever imagined. He won't shit for days. He simply doesn't have the muscles. That's how bad it's gotten. Now, we give him Miralax every day with his meds, prune juice in his tube, Tabasco, salsa, and whatever else makes any average human race to the toilet, but it hardly makes a dent.

The most difficult part is that his body tells him he needs to shit at least ten times a day. That is, at least ten times a day I have to drive him to the bathroom, pull him up to the counter, step to the side of his chair, put my right hand under his right arm, wrap my left arm around his back and under his left arm, and pull him up like a power lifter and shove his head and shoulders into the sink so he can pseudo-stand up and I can get his shorts down to his ankles, and ask him if he's able to pseudo-stand on his own.

"Are you ok?"

He grunts.

"Say yes or no," I tell him so that I know for sure whether or not I can let go for a brief moment.

"Yes," or "I'm falling," is generally the answer. If Babette is with us she helps with the lifting, and it's much easier with two people, but I can still do it by myself because my father has just a tiny bit of strength left in his legs.

And when it's a "Yes" I step away from his bony legs, and his small wrinkled white ass, and as quick as I can I move his wheelchair out of the way and grab the shower chair and whip it around behind him, lock it into place and, putting my hands back under his arms, lower him as slowly as I can to the chair and then roll him over the toilet. Then he doesn't shit and I have to do it backwards to put him back in his wheelchair. Then he does it again immediately after that. But he does need to shit. His body knows it. He knows it. He just can't do it.

We've now graduated from the plastic toilet to the shower chair with a hole in it because my father can no longer wipe his own ass, and it's too dangerous to leave him lodged on the counter while I wipe him standing up.

Then we repeat this process about ten times a day.

It can get tense. Maybe my father says something that feels like he's telling me some way I'm doing something wrong (which is perfectly reasonable). Of course I react by telling him (but probably snapping at him) why I'm doing what I'm doing. He tells me not to start my bullshit again. This time I tell him that everything I do doesn't need a goddamn critique. He tells me not to pretend that I'm the victim. He tells me I should be in the fucking movies I'm so fucking dramatic. I wanna tell him that he's not the only victim, but I know I'm not really a victim, and I had planned the critique speech one time before while screaming to myself in the car, but it didn't go anything like I thought it would, so I just storm out and tell Babette that I can't fucking take it anymore and go to my room and lie on my bed for a couple minutes before she comes back and asks me to help get him off the toilet.

Eddie calls to see how I'm doing with cleaning the transmission.

"Checking on me?"

"Absolutely," he confirms. "What's the status of the tranny, sir?"

"Well, I've put a coat of the stuff all over it. And I can see the junk coming off even when I put the coat on, so it seems to be working. It's just sitting outside at the moment. I was gonna take a putty knife to it and see if it comes off."

"No, no, paint it one more time and put it out in the sun. Today's a nice day so just roll it out there and let the sun work on it. What's really gonna get it off is a little elbow grease." He had pointed to his elbow, I remembered from another Eddie lesson, and I suddenly realize I never knew what elbow grease actually was. It isn't grease at all.

I put another coat of Eddie's elixir on the tranny and roll it on the floor dolly out into the sunniest part of the carport.

Later in the afternoon, when the sun has passed over the front of the house and into the backyard, I sit down with some rags and a putty knife and go to work on the grease. It wipes off rather easily on the larger smooth parts. I use the brush Eddie had left for me to get around the curves and into the crevices. Scraping. Wiping. Brushing. Brushing. Wiping. Scraping. One side and then the next, until the 350 turns from mostly gunky black to a dull silver.

Babette opens the door so my father can roll out next to me. He parks next to the tranny.

"Well. I got most of it off, I think." I look up at my father.

He nods his head. "You sure did. I'm proud of you son."

It's a strange thing to hear from my father. Not that he isn't often proud. There isn't a prouder father. I know that very well. He just doesn't express himself like that.

"Business school?" he once answered me after I told him I had been accepted as a freshman to the University of Texas business school. "Every Tom, Dick, and Harry goes to business school." But I now know what he meant. Be bigger. Strive further. Push harder. He just says it backwards sometimes. And every Tom, Dick, and Harry pretty much does go to business school.

I make some small talk with him about engines and grease and get us inside before I start to cry.

I send Eddie an email that the tranny's cleaned.

My father's old and dear friend Eddie Okies flies in for the weekend to see him. Eddie and my father met each other in college at Texas Western after attending rival high schools in El Paso. Texas Western, now UTEP, is most famous for Don Haskins starting five black players against an all-white Kentucky basketball team in the 1966 NCAA National Championship title game, breaking barriers and paving some of the way for black athletes in all sports. Also, still the only Texas school to win the NCAA Basketball title.

They both ended up in Houston for school as my father went to law school and Eddie trained to be a heart surgeon under legendary cardiac surgeon Dr. Michael DeBakey. My father re-tells a story of the time Frank Sinatra called Eddie's hospital when his father needed a heart operation.

"Hello, this is Frank Sinatra," Mr. Sinatra said when Eddie answered.

"Oh yeah, and this is President Johnson!" replied young Eddie.

Eddie moved to Portland in the early seventies, but forty years later, even after hardly seeing each other, they were as close as they were in college. It was Eddie's car they drove as LBJ whizzed by them on the drive home though the Texas Hill Country.

Eddie and my father kept in touch over the years, more recently via Skype, but as my father deteriorated and was more unable to speak, Eddie decided to fly in and spend a weekend with us.

I meet him by the front gate and walk him into the house.

"I love you Blu," he says as soon as he sees my father, and leans over to his chair and gives him a big long hug.

"I love you too, Jokes. More than you know." My dad calls Eddie Jokies or Jokes.

"Well, I wouldn't be here otherwise," Eddie says.

"Fuck you!" my dad replies.

"Ah, there! That's better!" And they laugh together.

Seeing Eddie always feels like I'm seeing one of my own old friends. Babette comes in and gives Eddie a hug and we all sit down and catch up. Eddie tells us about what he's doing since he retired. About his daughter's recent wedding and about his wife's new job at Nike.

We call Eddie's sister and all go to Cracker Barrel for breakfast. It's a good day and my father hasn't talked as much in months.

Eddie comes with us that evening to our monthly support group meeting with other ALS sufferers and caretakers from the West Texas and Southern New Mexico area. We've come to love our support group. You can meet people like yourself. You can get advice. You can get equipment. You can get a little sanity. It's one of our favorite times of the month. We get together with a few other folks like ourselves and have a few drinks, a good Mexican dinner, and talk a bit.

When I walk into the room they have reserved for us at the restaurant, a younger girl (my age) hops up and gives me a hug. It takes me a minute to recognize Sondra from a meeting earlier in the summer. Her father Henry, a local drummer, had died the summer before. Then, a woman who could only be her mother comes right up to me and says, "Oh Blu, I've been wanting to meet you! It's so good what you're doing for your father. I'm Mary Kay. I've known your father since I was a young girl."

I sit down next to Sondra. Babette, Eddie, and my father follow. I introduce everyone.

Sondra's mom gets up and walks over to my father. She leans down to his ear.

"Do you remember the Jenkins, Blu?" she asks him.

"Yes I do," answers my father.

"Well, I'm Mary Kay Jenkins. I grew up right around the corner from you and the Ivys. We had a crush on you since we were little kids!"

My father smiles and laughs and raises his arms as high as he can. "I'll be darned," he says. Mary Kay leans down and gives him a big strong hug.

"Sorry Babette, but we did!"

"I hear it all the time!" Babette says laughing. "Who was your sister?" Babette asks Mary Kay.

"Madeline."

"Oh my gosh! I can't believe it. She was one of my best friends growing up!"

"Your brother was Dennis?" my father asks.

"Yes Dennis. He was the oldest."

They trade back and forth and pass a photo of Henry around the table.

"Everyone says it, but it really is a small world," Mary Kay says.

And we all agree.

Linda and Gene Ott are the patriarchs of the New Mexico support group. Linda is a silver-haired easy-going grandmother you could knock a few drinks back with. Gene is her round joker of a husband. A happy-as-can-be couple despite losing a daughter to ALS.

I walk around the table to say hi.

"I heard you got away for the holidays," Linda says to me.

"I did!" I answer. "My mom was in San Antonio visiting my sister. It was good. I hadn't seen her in almost a year."

"Well, that's great that you got to go."

"And I'm sneaking away to Jamaica next week to shoot a wedding," I add.

"That's even better!"

"Yeah, you know, everyone tells you you need a break. That you gotta do something for yourself. But for me it's just anxiety and wondering what's going on back home and if my dad's ok and all that stuff and I wind up just wanting get back home."

"Well, you end up needing them as much as they need you," she says to me and smiles.

A perspective I had never really considered.

This meeting a nutritionist speaks to the group. She hands out information on nutrition and speaks a bit about what she has read on nutrition and ALS. But that's one of the problems we face in our battle with this disease. Nobody really knows that much about it unless they've actually lived it, and most people simply have not. She makes a point about malnutrition and she talks a bit about feeding tubes.

Mary Kay stands up to say that her husband, Henry, made his peace with God and that he did not get a feeding tube.

Linda Ott stands up to tell the group that her daughter got a tube but never used it as a show of rebellion. The longer she went, the more she won.

And Eddie Okies stands up to let everyone know that indeed a feeding tube was a valuable tool for recovery in his cardiac surgery practice.

I hope to myself that the nutritionist will get a chance to spend time with ALS patients. I'm a believer that diet can be a helpful part of living with this disease. I'd like to see studies on the impact of a vegan/macrobiotic diet on ALS, but you won't see that, because there isn't any money in eating your vegetables. There's only money in drugs and everybody knows it.

I hear our wrought iron gate clang as Eddie Solis lets himself in. I wrap my dad in blankets to bring him outside. Eddie has a Ziploc bag in one hand and a giant watch-gear-looking wheel in the other.

"I went by Petey's place and got transmission seals," he tells me and my father and holds up the bag. "There are three of them. They were cheap. Three bucks."

Petey runs a parts shop and is an old acquaintance of both my father and Eddie.

He sets the giant watch-gear-thing on the ground, opens the bag and pulls out the transmission seals. "You have the front seal," he holds one up. "The rear seal," he holds a different one up. "And this one here for the shifter pawl."

"The what?"

"The shifter pawl. Right here," he points to what just looks to me like a metal rod sticking out of the side of the transmission.

"The shifter ball?"

"Pawl. P-A-W-L. It connects to where you do the shifting inside the car. Park. Drive. Reverse." "Now the rear seal goes here," Eddie points to the smaller pointed end of the transmission. "The shifter pawl seal goes here," he points to the shifter pawl. "and the front seal goes right here," he points inside the big bell end of the transmission where the torque converter fits. "And this is the one we need to be careful with, because when you connect the torque converter to the transmission, you don't want to break the seal. If you tear it, then you have an oil leak and all sorts of trouble. So what you want to do is practice putting the torque converter on before you actually do it. If you pick up the torque converter it fits on like this," he uses his hand like a steering wheel. "It has two motions. First you put it on the shaft, then you twist it and push, and you'll feel it click and slide into place. But you *cannot* touch that seal."

"Ok," I say. "Just twist and push."

"Exactly," he says. "Practice that, and then the next time I come back we'll seal it up. That'll take no time at all. Then we'll put the torque converter on. But before we do that we need to take off the manual transmission that's on there now."

"Is that difficult?"

"Not if you have an impact wrench."

"My money says we do."

"Ok good, then get the impact wrench out and take off the tranny. It's easy. You'll see the bolts. Put it on a floor dolly and don't tip it over. And there's one other thing we need. The bolts for the flywheel."

A flywheel, I learn, is a big wheel that indeed looks like a giant watch gear that goes between the torque converter and the engine. Eddie tells me we'll go bolt hunting soon, leaves the flywheel with me, and with the day's lesson complete, heads home.

Eddie Okies comes by for lunch and I run some errands.

When I return, he and my father are in front of the computer watching YouTube videos of a man named Richard Feynman. Feynman was a famous quantum physicist who died in the eighties, but I had never heard of him. Eddie's was big fan and he and my dad are watching a series of interviews with him. Feynman, from what I could gather, was a jokester genius. He was always smiling and seemed genuinely excited about every little thing in the world. And I do mean every little thing, since quantum physics is the study of the most minute parts of our universe. Parts that no one can really see and that most people, me included, can't really understand.

But there's one particular interview where Feynman says something that strikes my father and me. After Eddie leaves for the day, my dad has me find it and replay it again for him. When being asked the ultimate question about humanity and nature, "Why are we here?" Feynman had this to say:

"I can live with doubt and uncertainty and not knowing...I think it's much more interesting to live not knowing than to have answers which might be wrong...I don't feel frightened by not knowing things."

Now here is a man who knows more about the inner workings of just about everything in the universe than any other person in the universe and he is plainly dismissing the fact that he doesn't actually know the reason we live and breathe, and more than that, he's saying he doesn't really care. It doesn't seem to bother him one bit. It's as trivial as any other miscellaneous question to him. He even goes on to say that he actually thinks we mean nothing. That our existence is merely a blip on the universal radar. A cosmic grain of sand. That we might as well have not existed as much as we existed.

When it comes to God or the lack thereof he just doesn't seem to mind. But that's strangely square in the middle of this man, by virtue of studying what he studies, caring more than anyone else in the world could possibly care. It's just that an unanswerable question doesn't seem to ruffle his feathers. Whereas for me, an unanswered question like that is torture. If I lie in bed and consider eternity, or preternity (my own word), it actually frightens me. Yet simultaneously it's the only thing that gives me hope. The fact, and it is a fact, that we truly do not know what's next, or what's further, or even what's infinitely inside us, makes me think that if anything, the possibility exists that there is something else meaningful for us. If we learn from the past and the past has value, and we are aware and value the present, then shouldn't the future also have value?

For my father, a man like Feynman essentially validates what he has thought most of his entire life. That when his body becomes only a body, and his breath is no longer, then it is indeed the end. No Heaven. No next. Simply nothing at all. My father is an Atheist, and his son is an admission away from being an Atheist. And although my dad will look up into the sky after telling a story about his mother and say "Where are you Mom?", it's a rhetorical question. He has no fucking idea where she is.

Babette once mentioned a time at a support group meeting, that I didn't attend, when my father talked to one of the speakers that evening and said something about how he had come to terms with God. The speaker had told Babette about it. I wouldn't call Babette particularly religious, but for the most part, and I certainly don't blame her, she believes that my father's suffering will end, and that he will indeed be in a place sans suffering after he dies. Now, I've often said to people, "What is a better place than with your wife and children that you love?" but I get the point. I have a hard time believing that my father had a come-to-Jesus moment, knowing as much as I know about his beliefs, but if he did, and I hope he found some way to cope with certain death, then I respect whatever it is that he found and I hope that it gives him comfort in a time where comfort is pretty hard to come by.

I wouldn't ever call myself full-blown Atheist because I wouldn't commit in either direction. I don't know as much as I know. Well, I don't know more than I know, but let's just call it I'm open to the possibility of something else. Most people call that an agnostic, but that's always a sort of a polite way of saying you mean Jesus and although I was raised a Catholic, or that is to say my mother was a Catholic and I went to Church with her, the only thing I've retained from those days gone by is a healthy dose of good old fashioned fear. Fear that no matter what my deeds, because I call bullshit on Jesus, my eyes will melt out of their sockets and I will die a hot hellacious (pun intended) death whereas my friend who fucked a hooker at his bachelor party will be playing a golden harp in a diaper sitting on a cloud when his time comes, and man, I just can't jive with that.

Eddie stays one more night and then his brother-in-law comes by to take him to the airport. I walk him to the gate and tell him how much my father loves him. We don't say it, but I think we both wonder if he'll ever see my father again.

Babette leaves the next day on a five day trip to Vegas with one of her childhood friends and her cousin. I'm happy to stay home with my dad and give her a chance to relax and hope that she enjoys herself.

When you're alone with my dad it's like there's a spring on your seat. Just when you think you can take a breath, or check your email, or just sit down, you have to get up. You have to scratch the left side of his nose. Then you sit. Then the right. Then you sit. Then he needs eye drops. Then you sit. Then you scratch his head. Then you sit. Then you check his email. Sit. Then you change the channel. Sit. Then you scratch his nose again. Sit. Then he has to use the bathroom. All relatively minor stuff, taken out of context, and, of course, only minor if you can use your arms and legs.

The first night we watch a shitty movie and go to bed late. My father decides to sleep on his side but that soon changes to his back when his left arm is too sore. His BIPAP alarm goes off several times in the first couple hours and we change once to his side again, once more back to his back, and once more to his side again over the next several hours. Around four in the morning he asks me to sit him up on the bed. I wrap a blanket around his back and sit in silence while he catches his breath. He asks me to put him in his chair where he finally falls asleep. I lie on his bed and doze in and out. Somewhere around six he asks me to put him back in bed on his side.

After he wakes up for good I get him out of bed and bundle him up in a blanket and we go into the garage to look at wrenches and sockets to get the manual transmission off of the engine. I pull out some sockets that look like strong sockets to me. They're black and I guess black looks strong.

"What are these?" I ask him.

"Those are for an impact wrench." he answers. Lucky guess. "You need to find out what size you need. Open the bottom drawer." he instructs, so I do. There are several air wrenches.

I pick one up. "This one?"

"No, you don't want that one. That's a ratchet."

"Ok, well, what's the difference?"

"Just keep looking."

I pull out another. "This one?"

My brother and my dad like to joke about how when my father asks me to get a screwdriver, I come back with a broom. I'm always good for a few laughs amongst handymen.

"That's a ratchet."

"Oh. This one?"

"That's the one. You might be able to use a ratchet but you really want the impact."

I wasn't completely wrong.

I grab the wrench, turn on the compressor, and pull the air hose all the way out to the transmission. He follows in his chair. We eye the bolts on the transmission housing and my dad guesses they're 9/16 and of course he's right.

I go back in and grab the 9/16 impact socket.

I put a floor dolly under the engine hanging on the cherry picker, and lower the engine onto the dolly so it will have some support and the transmission will stick off the front of the dolly where I can safely remove it. I put another small dolly underneath it to catch it after I take it off.

I put the socket on the impact wrench and pull the trigger.

"VRRIMMM! VRRIMMM!" It makes the exact sound it makes in a tire store or a NASCAR pit stop. I kinda hope the neighbors hear so it sounds like I'm doing something they can't do.

With the wrench it takes almost no effort at all to get the bolts off the transmission. The tranny is a bit heavy but once the bolts are off it slides right off the two pins that hold it steady on the engine. I settle it down onto the floor dolly below. I push the tranny out of the way, my dad and I go inside and I text Eddie that the tranny is off.

On a Sunday my dad and I watch the NFL playoffs. Neither one of us are rabid football fans, but I find myself craving Saturdays and Sundays in front of the TV. Maybe because it's something for us to do that changes a little bit every week.

I make my dad an English muffin with butter and jelly, but he salivates too much and can't eat it, so I make him eggs. He chokes twice on the eggs and spits them up all over his shirt and asks me to just put some Ensure in his feeding tube. A signpost, if you will. Foreshadowing. And we both know it.

After the first football game we decide to go to the mall because my dad wants to get some new sheets for his bed. El Paso has a knack for businesses going out of business but the mall is so empty I can't help but think it's just a sign of the times. It's almost sad walking around what feels like a ghost town.

We look through the slim Ralph Lauren sheet selection and decide on some maroon sheets and three new blankets for my dad. Not that we need any more blankets but I guess since it's part of my dad's wardrobe now he deserves some new duds.

My dad knows his suit style. He wore great suits to the courthouse. He was very strict on the rules. From sleeves to ties, my brother and I always consulted our father for advice. But there are no dress clothes to buy today. All his suits now sit in those vacuumed space-saver bag things in a closet.

I walk and he rolls towards the food court so we can grab a bite to eat. I figure it's more of a hassle than it's worth to find and use the elevator so he waits downstairs while I get us both corn dogs and cherry lemonades from Corn Dog on a Stick. We sit in the big open area where kids get their photos with Santa during the holidays and eat. We don't say much other than to say that these are damn good corn dogs. My father doesn't choke. It's a good lunch.

That night we watch half of The Wrestler but my dad says it's too damn depressing and that if he wants to be depressed he'll just look at himself.

The next morning Eddie Solis and Johnny drop by to look at the tranny. Eddie informs me that the tranny is actually not completely off, which of course does not surprise me, and that I still need to take off the clutch, which I didn't realize was on there in the first place. So, I get the impact wrench back out and with a little help from Johnny take off another five or so bolts that hold the clutch. It takes just a few minutes to get all the bolts off and I set the clutch down on a pallet by the engine.

Eddie and Johnny head back home and my dad and I go inside and watch some TV, interrupted only by my dad asking for the back scratcher…and you know what that means.

The next night we go eat oysters, my dad's all-time favorite meal, with Frank Ivy, one of my dad's childhood neighbors. Frank has recently moved back to El Paso from Austin where he was a successful attorney, complete with an ad on the back cover of the phone book, to care for his ailing father. He drops by from time to time to have lunch. Frank is twenty-five years sober but you sometimes feel like he's twenty-five seconds from falling off the wagon. He's a talker like many of my sober friends. As if they're doing everything they can to keep their mind off using.

Frank informs me at the table that my dad, "got more pussy than anyone I've ever known." A true compliment indeed among male friends.

My dad eats oysters with ease because they just slide down his throat. No chewing. I love that he can eat them and I love even more how much pleasure I know he gets out of eating them.

My father almost sleeps the entire night. Babette comes back home the next day and we have a few days of teamwork before I leave for Jamaica.

It's thirty degrees back home and Jamaica is warm and the water is beautiful. It's a long bus ride through what's very clearly the third world from the airport to the resort. People standing on the side of the road, some waving, some giving us the finger. We stay at a Sandals resort, which is more or less like a cruise ship on land. Most patrons look terrible in a bathing suit and are older than our group on average by probably twenty years. One American tourist at the bar has somehow wound up with a stash full of Miller Lites, which the bartender tells me he has actually packed and transported from America, as you can only get Red Stripe on the resort.

We get settled on a Thursday, and on Friday morning my brother, who has flown in to take my place, emails me to tell me they took my father to the emergency room because he wasn't breathing well. I keep it a secret from the wedding patrons not wanting to take any of the focus off of the bride and groom. They put my father on a hospital BIPAP for several hours, do tests, and send him home as they could really do nothing for him. I know he's frightened and uncomfortable and I wish I could be there to rub his neck or just sit by his bed.

My brother says they went for Italian food at my dad's favorite Italian restaurant, The Italian Kitchen, but my father was unable to swallow and gave up early in the meal.

I call that night. My brother puts me on speaker.

"Hi Dad."

"Hi Son," he garbles.

"I heard you took a trip today too."

"Yeah." I can barely understand him.

A bit of silence.

"Well, I love you and I'll be home soon ok?"

"Ok, Son. How are your photos?" My dying father, fresh out of the hospital, who can barely get a sentence out, is asking me about my photography.

"Good Dad. So far so good. I'll email you a few when I get some good ones."

I can't hear the rest. My father sounds so weak. Like he's barely there.

I once wrote this chorus to a song:

> I hope you're in paradise
>
> Away from this fucked up miserable life
>
> Long sandy beaches yeah that would be nice
>
> Paradise

My brother keeps me posted on the rest of his weekend, which is a variation of all of my weekends. They tried to shit ten times a day. It was constant work helping my dad. He choked a lot. And on occasion they laughed together.

While I'm at DFW on the way back home, Willie texts that his brother has died in what sounds like a car accident. I tell him to come by soon and that my dad would love to see him and we are all thinking of his family and if he needs anything to please call us.

"I'll never forget you all," he texts back.

The El Paso Times website says his brother was murdered in a gas station argument at two in the morning. They drove over his body in the parking lot.

My dad was too weak to go to the funeral.

I come home after five days to yet another man in my father's body. His white beard has grown. He's skin and bones. He can barely talk. I lean over and kiss his forehead. I hug his bony shoulders.

"A rough flight," I tell him. They shut down DFW that night after my flight. It's gonna be single digits in El Paso in a couple days. My father seems happy I'm home.

We stay inside for most of the next several days as it's just too damn cold for us to go anywhere. My father's frustration is growing. One night as we watch a movie he has me turn his chair towards his computer and he just stares at the black screen.

Eddie Solis emails:

>Junkyard hunting for bolts will not be fun but we will do it.

>Get a filler tube with a dipstick.

>Also the kick down cable. Should be about fifteen dollars for this item.

>When you have the above in hand, let me know, I will provide a little more guidance.

>Bossy aren't I?

I do a first edit on my Jamaica photos and show them to my father. "I guess I didn't realize Jamaica was south of Cuba. We musta flown right over it."

"They won't let you," he informs me in a whisper.

"Like you can't fly in their airspace?"

"Right," another whisper.

"Have you ever been to Cuba?" I ask him. I'm ashamed I don't even know the answer to this.

"Twice," he says and then something else I can't make out.

"Tell me again," I say to him.

"I can't talk," he often tells me and tries to motion to his mouth.

"You spend half your breath telling me that you can't talk Dad. Just tell me again."

He continues, frustrated. "We went twice on the ship," Pause. "for exercises."

A longer pause.

He continues. "Some of the Cubans," Pause. "would work on the base."

"You mean some of the Cubans from Cuba were actually allowed on the base?"

"Yes. I remember," Pause. "seeing them open the gate," Pause. "and they would come in," Pause. "eight to five," Pause. "and then back out the gate." Pause. "I always thought it was strange."

"That does sound strange. They should just let people go to Cuba. It's stupid. I don't get it."

My dad naps in his wheelchair. When he wakes up we watch a Chuck Berry documentary. There's a shot in the movie with a parking lot of (what are now) classic cars.

"Look at all those cars," I say to him and the TV.

My dad nods. "I was there."

I meet Eddie for coffee and to go bolt hunting and discuss our plans.

It's one of the coldest days on record for El Paso. One degree. Our house manages to survive with heat and power but others aren't as lucky. There are frozen pipes and gas shortages all over town. The city is on a water alert. You're not supposed to use your dishwasher, or your washing machine, or even bathe unless it's absolutely necessary. If you want to drink out of the tap you're instructed to boil the water first.

Starbucks is packed. We sit down on some cushiony brown leather seats. A former architect roommate of mine told me once that Starbucks designs their stores so that they look inviting, but that they're actually not comfortable enough to make you stay very long. I wonder if that's true.

Eddie asks about my mother. He says that he never felt comfortable asking about her around my father. I thank him for asking and tell him she's still teaching elementary school in Ohio and doing well. We finish our coffee and walk to the parking lot. Eddie hassles me about my Obama bumper sticker on the way out.

"Where are we headed?" I ask him.

"Transmission shops."

We drive east on I-10 and talk about Juarez as we pass it on our right.

A-Tree is the shop run by Petey. The store itself is like a small warehouse, dimly lit with high ceilings and shelf after shelf of parts. The walls are a light green and it's ice cold as there doesn't seem to be heat in the building.

"Mr. Petey!" Eddie says as we walk in the door.

In an accent very similar to the late Ricardo Montalban, the man at the counter replies, "No, no, Mr. Solis, I am Javier. But I forgive you."

"Javier! Of course." Eddie laughs a bit. "I knew that. I don't know why I just called you Petey. Please accept my apology."

"Apology accepted. What can I do for you Mr. Solis?"

"Well, we're hoping you can help us. We have a Turbo Hydramatic 350 and we're looking for some parts." Eddie explains.

"I can help," Javier assures us. "What is it that you need?"

"The first thing we need is a flywheel."

Javier turns and walks away towards a shelf. "There are two flywheels for the 350," he says over his shoulder. "A big one…and smaller one." He grabs a wheel and brings it to the counter. "Do you know which one it is?"

"We have the torque converter," Eddie offers and motions me to go grab it.

"Well, certainly bring it in," he says, and I walk outside to my truck and bring in the heavy cold torque converter and set it on the counter. A torque converter sort of looks like a pound cake pan with a lid on it. I have yet to learn how it actually converts torque or if it even does that at all.

Javier hands Eddie the flywheel and lifts the torque converter up on its side. Eddie holds the wheel up to the converter.

"You have to measure the distance between here," Javier points to a bolt hole, "and the carburetor."

We had already tried and failed to fit the flywheel Eddie had brought over to the house, so Eddie's best guess is that this smaller one would do the trick. "I think this one will do," he says.

"Ok," acknowledges Javier. "What else do you need?"

"Do you have a dipstick and filler tube?"

Javier walks to a different shelf. "This should work," and he hands a long plastic package to Eddie. Eddie sets it on the counter.

"Excellent. And how about a kick down cable?"

Javier goes to another shelf and brings back another long package. "Now, there are two types of cables that can work. See if this one works and if not there is another one," he hands it to Eddie.

"You wouldn't happen to have the bolts to bolt the flywheel to the crank, would you?" Eddie asks.

"No. Unfortunately I do not." Javier answers politely.

"Alright then," Eddie looks at me. "Do we have anything else?"

I pull my phone out and look at the list I had made. "I think that's it."

Javier gathers the parts together and I pay for them with a credit card.

"Ok Mr. Javier. We thank you very much for your help."

Javier nods his head gratefully, "Yes sir. And I'll tell Petey you say hello."

Eddie then directs me from A-Tree down the street, through an alley to avoid a one-way, and back around the block to park in front of another car shop.

"These are hard bolts to come by, no?" I ask Eddie.

"Apparently so. It's going to be one of those things where someone picks up an old hubcap full of bolts and happens to have them in the pile, but we'll find 'em."

We get out and go inside, careful not to slip on the ice on the sidewalk.

At the counter is a Mexican man with no front teeth bundled in several layers of warm clothes with a sweatshirt hood over his head. The store is bitterly cold. You can see your breath. No heat seems to a recurring theme. There is a younger kid to his right. The shop smells of something cooking.

In Spanish, Eddie asks the man about the bolts. I understand most of the words. My Spanish is always better with context. The man does not have the bolts but suggests we go to the shop two doors down on the corner and ask there.

As we turn to walk away I notice an actual BBQ grill behind the counter. It's on for heat, and that's why the place smells like food.

Sun City Auto Service is on the corner. We walk in the door. There's a man at the counter on the phone facing away from us. Eddie grabs him on the shoulders and shakes him a bit to let him know he's there. The man reaches back without turning around and shakes his hand like he knows who he is by instinct. He puts the phone to his chest and calls someone in from the shop without turning around.

Another bundled-up man comes to the door and shakes Eddie's hand. Eddie seems to know everyone in this part of town. This man looks older. His teeth aren't much better than the last guy's and he has a big red bulbous nose like he's a drinker. He's bundled up in a hood too. Eddie asks him again in Spanish about the bolts.

He leads us through the ice cold shop, around a few workers, and over some car parts. We step over a hitch to a trailer with a boat on it, around a couple of cars and to a shed in the back of the yard. And sure enough, the man pulls out a pan of all sorts of miscellaneous nuts and bolts and starts to sort through them.

But after sifting through the pan a bit it's clear that he isn't gonna find what we're looking for. In Spanish he tells Eddie something that I don't quite catch. He shakes both of our hands and leads us back through the maze of cars and into the front office. The man on the phone at the counter turns around and silently mouths a hello and goodbye to both of us.

We navigate carefully around the ice on the sidewalk again and back to the car. "Well, it was exactly like you predicted. A pile of bolts in a hubcap."

"I thought we were gonna get lucky," Eddie admits. "There's one more place we need to try."

He directs me through a warehouse district of sorts, not too far from the car shops, to the front of a small junkyard. I thought it interesting to find a junkyard right in the middle of town.

"Hopefully we'll be in luck," Eddie says as we get out of my truck and walk towards the gate.

The junkyard looks like most junkyards look, if you've ever been in a junkyard, just a little smaller. Wrecked cars everywhere. Some on top of the other. In various states of disassembly. A barrel with a fire off to our left. A pile of transmissions and torque converters at our feet when we walk in the gate.

The owner walks in the distance out of ear shot. After he passes in view once or twice more he sees us and makes his way to the front.

Eddie shakes his hand and introduces us. "We're hoping you can help us out of a bind."

"Ok," the man answers. "What do you need?"

"Well, we're looking for the bolts for a TH350 flywheel that connect to the crank."

"Not the bolts for the torque converter?"

"Not those. We have those, but the other bolts are proving to be a bit hard to find."

The man looks off into the yard as if he's thinking. "I tell you what, why don't you call me later this afternoon. I think I have them on a car in here, but call me later and I'll let you know."

"Sounds great," Eddie says. "I'll call you in a few hours." We all shake hands, and we leave.

"He's got em," Eddie says to me confidently.

"You think so?"

"Yeah, he's got em."

My dad takes a shit after at least an entire week.

Days pass. They are regular days. We watch The Military Channel. A movie at night. My father hardly eats.

Eddie calls to say he has a present for me. He's outside calling from the driveway. He lets himself in the gate and then the side door and hands me a Ziploc full of bolts.

"Ah, you got em!" I say excitedly.

"I told you he'd have them."

"Fantastic. Should we put em on?"

"Do you have the flywheel handy?"

"Of course!"

Eddie pokes his head into the living room and says hi to my father. My uncle and my father's friend Butch are over having lunch. A combination of Bill, Butch, Vince, and the occasional tag-along come to eat lunch at the house at least two or three times a week these days, and we look forward to each one. My father hardly eats but he laughs and listens and that is more than enough.

We walk outside to have a look. I open the garage and grab the flywheel from my growing pile of parts. Eddie takes the wheel and places it up to the end of the engine. He lines up the holes on the shaft to the holes on the flywheel and says, "Yep, that's the one."

I empty the bag of bolts onto the ground. There are six black bolts along with six washers that look like a sorta round star, called tooth washers. I pick a bolt up and twist it into the first hole. It goes right in.

"Now, these bolts are gonna need to be torqued. Do you have a torque wrench?" he asks me.

"Well," I vaguely remember what a torque wrench looks like, "probably. Tell me what a torque wrench is and that'll be a good start."

"A torque wrench," Eddie explains, "is a wrench that measures the foot pounds of pressure, or some other measurement I can't recall right now, you need to apply to a bolt when turning it. It looks like a ratchet but it has a gauge or a dial on it and as you turn the bolt it tells you how much torque you are applying. You need a specific pressure depending on what you're doing. John Attel I'm sure can tell us how much these bolts need."

I send John a quick text.

"How many foot pounds for the bolts that hold the flywheel to the crank?"

"65/70" is the quick reply.

"Thank you sir," I text back.

"Ok, and one more thing," Eddie says, "as you tighten the bolts, the flywheel is going to turn. Do you have a flathead screwdriver?"

"Sure, lemme grab it." I walk over to the drawer labeled "screwdriver" and grab the biggest flathead I can find.

I hand it to Eddie and he shows me how I can anchor the screwdriver between the cogs on the flywheel and a smaller cogged wheel that's on the starter to stop the wheel from turning while I tighten the bolts.

"Now, how does the starter work exactly? I mean, what does it actually do to start the car?" I ask him.

"The starter, " he says, "engages with power from the battery and the little wheel you see there." He points to the small cogged wheel which looks like a tiny flywheel that sits inside a cylinder on the side of the transmission. He continues, "That wheel moves forward and locks into the flywheel. When it turns, the flywheel turns. Then once it moves the flywheel it pulls back and disengages."

"Ah. Ok. I get it." I don't truly get it, but I get the order of operations at least. "Lemme ask my dad about the torque wrench."

I walk inside and call out to my dad. "Hey Dad, do we have a torque wrench?"

He looks in the air like he's thinking. "Well I do," Pause. "But I don't know *where* it is." In my head I can hear the accent on the "where." He gives me a look. A look that says someone besides him put his torque wrench somewhere in the garage even though no one in this house has any good reason to use his torque wrench. My dad loves to pretend that everyone besides himself loses all his things.

"What did you do with my keys?" he'd ask me over the phone.

"Well, I don't know, Dad. I'm in college. I live in Austin."

"Snap-On," he suggests. There are two tool boxes in the garage. An old gray and red Snap-On tool box, and a bigger, newer redder Snap-On that's sitting in front of the gray one. I check the top, which is mostly sockets, and then check the big bottom drawer where I quickly find what looks like a cross between a ratchet and a meat thermometer.

I bring it to him. "This it?"

He nods.

Butch and Bill get up to leave and I wrap my dad in a brown blanket up to his neck. I take the controls so he can keep his arms under the blanket and wheel him outside. I set him in a patch of sun on the carport. In the desert there's a big difference between the shade and the sun.

"Just torque the bolts and I'll come back by tomorrow and we'll seal the tranny and marry it up to the engine," Eddie says.

"I think I can do that."

Doug pokes his head in the gate to see what we're up to. I'm fiddling with the screwdriver to stop the flywheel while I turn the bolts. He shows me the proper place to jam it in and tells me to tighten the bolts opposite each other and never one next to the other, similar to what you would do if you were changing a tire. As I turn the torque wrench I watch the gauge move from zero to twenty to thirty-five to sixty to seventy. Doug wanders back to his house and my dad watches me tighten up the rest of the bolts.

It's an easy day's work and we go inside to get warm.

The next morning Eddie comes by early with a bag of tools.

My dad's awake so I wrap him up again and bring him outside to watch. I open the garage and pull out our big rolling workbench that my dad had Carlos make out of a solid door and some of the angle steel from the trailer. I clean a spot and lift up the tranny and put it on the bench.

Eddie pulls out what he calls a seal puller, which looks like a small pick axe, and shows me in the air how to pull the seal out of the transmission. "You lodge it in the middle of the seal, and rock it back and forth. Careful not to scrape the aluminum. Rock it and pull."

I lean into the tranny and put one corner of the puller into the right side of the seal and sort of rock it and sort of pull it. "I'm not sure how hard to pull!"

"Just pull it!"

I rock and pull a little harder. Then a little harder. The seal moves slightly. A little more and then it pops out, still hanging on the puller.

"You see! A little elbow grease." Eddie smiles at me. "Now. Get the new seal, and grab a hammer." I walk over to the hammer cabinet and show a couple of hammers to Eddie until he sees one he likes. Then he pulls out a long cylinder-looking thing and says, "Ok. Put the new seal in and I'll hold this here." He puts the cylinder up to where the seal will fit. "Put the seal in, I'll put this over the seal, and then knock this end with your hammer. Try to do it evenly. We want the seal to go in even."

I position the seal, Eddie puts the seal installer against the seal, then I rear back and...tap the hammer lightly against the cylinder.

Eddie gives me a look. "Maybe a little more power," he says sarcastically, and I knock the cylinder until the seal starts to move into place. I hit the top, the bottom, the center, and each side a few times as it gradually works its way into its new home.

I look back at Eddie. "I'm guessing pros can knock these things in with one or two shots?"

"That is correct sir."

We turn the transmission around and do the same thing on the back seal. Then we move to the side of the tranny to the shifter seal. I disassemble the shifter (turn a screw) and put the parts in a plastic bag. I've been bagging and labeling all my pieces. I try to put the seal puller in the shifter shaft but it's too big. "I don't think it's gonna get in there," I say to Eddie.

He takes the puller and has a go at it. "I think you might be right. There's a seal remover for the shifter seal, and I know I have one somewhere but I thought we'd have luck with this one. Very well, then we'll have to get ourselves a shifter seal remover!"

"Looks like it."

Eddie asks for some grease, which I can't find, and then for Vaseline, which I find inside the house. He has me grease up the stub of the converter which connects to the transmission. I lift the torque converter off the ground, and lay it up against the transmission.

"Remember your moves," Eddie instructs me.

I put the converter on the shaft, turn and push it. It moves forward. Then I rock it back and forth and I push a little more and it slides right on and into place with almost no effort at all.

"Well done!" Eddie congratulates me.

I look at my dad, "Not bad, minus all the anxiety." My dad smiles and nods his crooked head.

I wheel him from the shade into the sun and turn him to face us.

Eddie pulls out a fancier-looking torque wrench and re-checks the torque on the flywheel. He gives the bolts a quick extra small turn. Then we go back to the workbench and together pick up the transmission and move it down in front of the engine. I pick up the engine with the cherry picker to position it up against the transmission. After a bit of adjusting we secure the two holes on the bell housing onto the knobs on the engine block. Putting on the housing bolts is relatively simple. We have a tranny on the engine. I look over to my father who has fallen asleep in the sun.

Eddie sends an email later in the evening:

> Seals and torque converter went well. The shift shaft seal can be replaced in or out of the car, just takes a few seconds with the correct tool. Send the alert when the adaptor kit arrives.
>
> Go ahead and remove the exhaust. We'll need a new one.
>
> Start spraying some WD-40 or similar product on the rear end u-bolts in anticipation of its removal.

Ohio

Wrap your brown hair around me

Push your body against mine

Protect me from the snow

Shield me from the wind

Hide me from the cold

Wait with me 'til spring

Jen kisses me at the baggage claim like a girl might kiss a boy in an airport, except I am totally unsure about it and probably pull away. I've had little to no female contact since I've been home. There just isn't any time for it. For commitment. For anything.

Brandi brought her freckles for my birthday the year before. At a friend's that night I left my phone in the kitchen with the ringer off only to pick it up after a few glasses of wine to missed call after missed call from Babette and a panicked text message that simply said, "HELP." My father had fallen as she tried to help him onto the toilet and he was wedged on the floor between it and the shower wall and she couldn't get him up. That was only a month into being home and more or less set the stage for the next seventeen.

Jen was different. I'd known her for years. She was smart, and funny, and attractive. Had long brown hair like my mother. I feel like I've read that men choose women like their mother. She even lived in Ohio.

My family has always been laid back as guests go. No one has ever been pressured to get married or to have children. Bringing someone home, although rare, was never that big of a deal. For me now, it's simply the only way I can spend any time with anyone.

Jen takes photos of me working on the car. The only real photos I have of me working.

I set the baby monitor near the bed and Jen undresses. I lie on my stomach. I can smell the massage oil as she takes it out of her bag.

To have hands on me. To be next to someone. It has been far too "WHEEP WHEEP! WHEEP WHEEP! WHEEP WHEEP!" goes the motherfucking breathing machine.

"ARRGH!" I muffle into my pillow. "I'll be right back," I sigh as I lift my head up, roll off the bed, hop into some shorts and run downstairs to make sure my father is breathing.

I race back up the stairs, undress, and launch myself back onto the bed.

"Ok. I'm sorry," I say to Jen behind me.

"Don't be sorrWHEEP! WHEEP! WHEEP! WHEEP!"

"Fuck."

Back downstairs. Back upstairs. Exhale. Face down. "Ok."

The machine gives us some time.

I sink into the "WHEEP! WHEEP! WHEEP! WHEEP!"

I hate the breathing machine. Hate it. HATE IT.

The alarm goes off another two or three or four or it doesn't really matter times.

"Let's just go downstairs." Jen suggests kindly but frustratingly as she puts her massage oils away and covers herself up.

Defeated, I agree.

I'm not sure what it was. The circumstance. The timing. The anxiety. Me. Her. Either way, Jen leaves a few days later because she has to go back to work and I don't ask her to stay.

The motor mounts come in after a week and half of being delayed. I eBay a shifter seal removal tool and a dust cover for the bottom of the TH350. Things are beginning to take shape.

Eddie comes by to look at the motor mount kit. We walk and wheel out into the cold.

"Looks good. How much did you pay for it?"

"Two hundred."

"That's not too bad for all this steel," he says and walks over to the '41. He lifts the hood and looks down into the empty space where the engine will go. Confirming in his head where the mounts will sit.

"Does it look right?" I ask him.

"Oh yes," he points down to the frame. "The left side should mount somewhere around there. And the right around there."

"And will we have to cut that bar?" I guess and point to the piece of the frame that goes from left to right behind the engine and under the car where I was told we'd have to cut by the guy at Chassis Engineering.

"Yes," Eddie confirms. "We'll cut it out and then we'll put the engine in and see where the mounts line up. We'll mark the holes. Drill 'em, and tighten it up."

Sounds easy enough, although I know it won't be.

"You need to clean," Pause. "that engine." Pause. "You can't," Pause. "put it in like that." Says my dad who hates assembling dirty anything.

"I will, I will," I assure him.

"And get a new," Pause. "valve cover." Pause. "Chrome."

That night we drive to get oysters, which my father will choke on and never eat again.

"Radar Love" by Golden Earring comes on the radio.

My dad whispers something I can't make out from the passenger seat.

"What?" I turn and look towards him.

"TURN. IT. UP," he repeats as loudly as he can.

I nod and crank the radio with a grin.

We blast "Radar Love" all the way home from the restaurant.

The next morning Eddie arrives with a different bag of tools, a drill, and some drill bits. He sits down at the engine, takes off the valve cover and has a look at a bolt that's stuck in a bolt hole that will hold the valve cover down.

"These can be a pain in the ass," he says. "Do you have a dental pick?"

"A dental pick? Like for your teeth?"

"Exactly."

I go to my dad's bedroom where he's still sleeping and take the dental pick that's on his bed table and bring it out to Eddie.

"Don't tell my dad."

"I won't," he laughs.

Eddie uses the dental pick to slowly turn the bolt in the block. The fine dental pick is just enough to grab a ridge on the broken bolt and turn it ever so slightly.

"I think we're in luck," he says without looking up. "I don't think we'll have to drill. These things can be terrible to get out. And even worse if they're on the bottom!" he points underneath the block and I imagine myself under the car trying to extract the bolt like an idiot.

Eddie tells me again to spray the u-bolts, so I crawl under the car on my back and look around the wheels until I see what have to be u-bolts and give them a good spray of WD40, though these bolts are more square than U.

I crawl out from under the car, Eddie stands up, and together we take the hood off of the '41, set it aside, and look down into the empty space where the original 216 engine once was. There's dust, and cables, and wires, and things that I don't know what they are.

"Your job is to cut the crossmember from there," he points to one side of the frame, "to there. And be careful not to cut anything else."

The old crossmember on the frame is a small bar that supported the old transmission. The new transmission is much wider, longer, and heavier than the old one. The old crossmember won't support the weight and size of the new transmission.

"Well, the good and bad news is, I don't really know what anything else is. I just don't wanna cut something I'm not supposed to cut."

Eddie blesses me with the sign of the cross. "Just cut," he says, "And call me when you're done."

The cold winter retreats into a mild March and makes way for what surely will be another beautiful El Paso Spring. I fly to Nashville to shoot another wedding and my brother comes in to take my place.

"I can tell a difference," he texts.

"Yeah, I know."

"We got Casa J tonight. He didn't want anything. Sad."

They had gotten take out from our favorite Mexican restaurant and my father hadn't wanted to even try a bite.

I leave on a Friday afternoon and am back the following Sunday.

"How are you doing?" I ask my father.

"Ok," he says in a whisper.

"About the same?"

"Worse."

He's hardly speaking. It's like he lost his voice almost completely in seventy-two hours. He just doesn't have the air to get the sound out. He's using his breather.

The next few mornings are awful. As soon as he opens his eyes he panics, wants to sit up, and just sits with his head down while saliva pours out of his mouth and onto his beard.

"What's going on?" I ask him.

"I don't know goddammit."

On no particular morning, after I get my father situated in his chair and watching the Military Channel, I put on my work boots, a pair of dirty jeans, and a long sleeve Dickies work shirt, and get my tools together for a day of grinding the frame. I drag an extension cord and the air compressor hose from the garage out and under the car. Then I get the creeper (the flat rolling cart that you lie on to roll yourself under a car), a headlamp, my safety glasses, an air chisel to knock some of the gunk out from under the car, some ear muffs to protect my hearing, a few wrenches in case I have to turn a few bolts, a mallet in case I have to hit something, some pliers, and a four inch grinder with a new metal grinding wheel, and push myself underneath the '41.

The car is quite high off the ground and easy to roll under. Doug told me that it's because there is no engine in it. I look upside down at the part of the frame that I need to cut out. There's a metal tube of some sort running the length of the crossmember. I follow it back to the rear wheels. Eddie said I might see brake lines, so I assume it's a brake line.

I reach over to the air hose and pull it up to my chest. I grab the air chisel and pop it on to the hose with a hiss of air. I put on my glasses and the ear muffs, and start chiseling greasy junk off of the frame. The air chisel is really, REALLY loud. The air chisel chiseling against metal is really, REALLY, REALLY loud. The metal brake line is hooked to the frame with a simple metal tab. I reach for my pliers and pull the tab until it snaps. With a little bit of a tug, the brake line comes away from the frame far enough, I think, to not be in the way of the grinder. But I also determine that I'll probably need to come at the frame from the engine side to get a good crack at it. I push my tools off to the side and scoot back towards the engine cavity. When

I'm inside the hole, I'm able to sit up and have a proper look at the work I have in front of me.

The left side where I need to cut looks fairly straightforward. The right side where I need to cut is right next to what looks to me to be something to do with steering. I'll try and not cut whatever it is in half while I'm grinding.

I reach for the grinder, get my balance, turn it on, and put it to the metal. Sparks fly. I can feel them hit my forehead. The grinder bounces. I push against it. It pushes back. I stop. There's a dent. It's grinding through the metal. I try again. Push further. Cut more metal. But as I get a little further into the frame it becomes clear that the four inch grinder isn't big enough to get through the thickness of the entire frame. Once you get about an inch in, the body of the grinder hits the frame and you have to stop. So I put the grinder down and decide I'll go get the nine inch grinder my dad bought last summer for...well just to buy a nine inch grinder. I'd used the nine inch grinder before, and it was a heavy, unwieldy beast of a tool. I'm not looking forward to it but I'm gonna cut the frame no matter what, and I'm not gonna ask anyone for help.

The grinder is big and heavy. This time I go into the engine cavity through the top of the car, and sit down on the floor. I'm a little nervous. I pick up the grinder like a shot gun and brace my right elbow against my waist so it won't pull back into my face. I pull the trigger and dig in. The grinder snaps back at me, bounces from the crossmember to something above me and back down like a pinball before I let go of the trigger. It makes a groove in something I don't know the name of.

"Fuck," I say out loud.

Using a nine inch grinder in the engine compartment of a car I imagine is something like using a chainsaw in a closet. But it pushes right through the left side of the frame much more easily than the four inch and in not too much time I have the left side cut.

The right side is a little trickier. I have to sorta maneuver around the steering piece that's bolted onto the frame. It's an even tighter squeeze than the left. I try to bring it up from the bottom, at an angle from the side, and eventually just kinda close my eyes and slam the grinder straight in. And as soon as I'm through, the middle piece of the frame drops to the ground between my legs.

I take the four inch grinder and smooth out the cuts I've just made. Then I crawl out from under the car and use a floor jack to hold up the old drive shaft that has been resting on the crossmember.

I text Eddie, "The frame is cut."

"Beetle Shop," my dad whispers to me.

"Beetle Shop?"

"Yes."

"Beetle Shop what?" I have no idea what this means. My brother and sister and I joke about the way my father likes to start a conversation with one random word out of nowhere and it's up to you to figure out what he means. John F. Kennedy. Peanut butter. Or in this case, Beetle Shop.

"Phone," Pause. "Call Carlos," Pause. "Karmann Ghia."

My dad has a turquoise Karmann Ghia that he acquired a few years back from who knows where, and had given it to Carlos (a different Carlos) at the Beetle Shop, presumably to work on. It had sat undriveable in our front carport for several years and has been at the Beetle Shop for at least two. My dad wants me to go pick it up and bring it back home.

"Did he fix it?"

"You're gonna fix it."

"Oh ok," I laugh a little.

"Call Eddie," Pause. "and see if he can go with you."

"Well lemme get your phone."

We never really use my father's phone anymore. Most people know not to call it and of course my father can't use it.

The Beetle Shop is under the B's in my dad's contact list. I call the mobile number.

There's shuffling on the other end. "Bueno?" Someone answers in Spanish.

"Hi, is this Carlos?"

"Yes?" From the other side.

"Hi Carlos, this is Blu Sanders. I'm the son of uh, the other Blu Sanders."

"Oh yes yes! Hello. What can I do for you? How's your father?" Like he's been waiting for the call.

"Well, he's hanging in there," My standard response. "He wants me to come get the Karmann Ghia from you and bring it back to the house, so I just wanted to know when was a good time to come by."

"Of course, of course. You know your father never told me what to do with it. It's just been sitting right here. When do you want to come get it?"

"Will you be there this afternoon?"

"Any time after two. We take lunch from one to two. I'll bring it out for you. It's no problem."

I call Eddie to see if he can tag along to help me strap the car down on the trailer. He says of course and that Johnny is at his house and he can come along as well.

I put the trailer on the Suburban and drive to south El Paso to grab Eddie and Johnny. I recount my crossmember cutting story to the two of them. I think they get a kick out of hearing a story that they've told in one way or another over the years. We take the border highway past the south El Paso barrio and our dusty zoo on the edge of El Paso, down to Alameda Street, and pull up in front of the Beetle Shop. Eddie gets out to help me park. He waves me ahead a few car lengths and I straddle the curb and park along the street.

Carlos and a worker from the shop are already pushing the Karmann Ghia out into the street and towards the trailer. I hop out of the car and Johnny and I each grab a ramp from under the trailer (stored under each side) and secure them to the end of the trailer. I go back to help push. The car goes up the ramps and onto the trailer with no problem. We stop it in the middle and I reach into the car and pull the emergency brake.

"Hi Carlos," I introduce myself. "My father wanted me to tell you that he was sorry he couldn't make it out here himself. It's just too hard for him these days."

Carlos shakes his head. "Oh, I understand. Your father never told me what to do with the car. I was waiting but I never heard anything. Please tell him hello for me. Your father's a good man."

Johnny takes the lead on the straps and puts one strap from the front of the trailer to a hook under the front bumper, and another on the back of the trailer to a hook under the back bumper.

"Slooow muuusic," Johnny says to me.

"Slow music?" I ask back to him.

"Driiiive slow. You don't want the car joining us in the front seat."

"Ah."

"Slooow muuusic, " Eddie repeats. "What's the formula your brother uses Johnny?"

"Masa con fuerza es…cabron!" and they both belly roll with laughter.

"What's that mean?" I ask them both.

"It means, mass times strength equals…goddammit!"

I leave Eddie and Johnny at Eddie's house and tow the Karmann Ghia home. My father and Babette are on the back patio waiting to watch me drive into the yard.

I do a circle and back the trailer up between two trees near the back fence. It's a beautiful day. The turquoise car shines in the sun.

My father drives slowly in his chair out to meet me and Babette goes inside. We move around the car. I open the doors so he can see in. It's full of dirt and leaves from maybe the window being open for a long time. The seats are torn up. There are a few parts scattered inside. I know he wishes he could fix it. I wonder what he thinks as we work our way around the car. Is he sad? Does he think to himself that he'll never see it run? That he metaphorically won't ever see much of anything run? Does he look around the yard? Back at his home? Does he wonder what all that work was really worth? Does he think about me? Will he miss the sun? The dogs? The trees?

We stop by the pecan tree. I find a bucket and pick some pecans off the ground and put them in the bucket. I'll take them to the patio where I have another bucket of pecans.

We make our way back towards the house, stop under the mulberry tree near the patio, and turn to face the back fence. There is a breeze. We listen to the wind chimes hanging from the tree. I reach down and rub my father's arm and he closes his eyes. I tell him I love the sound of the wind chimes.

"Will you," Pause. "keep rubbing," Pause. "my arm like that?" he asks with his eyes closed.

"Like this?" I keep rubbing. "Of course."

I get a chair from the patio and sit next to him. He falls asleep in the breeze while I rub his skinny arm. I push the skin where his muscles used to be. I watch him breathe. I look at his beard. The chimes sing in the wind. Tears roll down my face and into the dirt below me.

Weeks go by. The weather stays good. My father gets worse.

We get a suction machine to suck the phlegm out of his mouth. I'm surprised he can even breath with everything that collects in his throat. You can also stick the suction tube up his nose and suck the snot out. Our living room begins to sound like a dentist's office.

My father stops eating and drinking through his mouth completely. We give him cans of Ensure and glasses of water through his feeding tube. He says even his taste buds have changed.

He also starts to insist that someone be in his bedroom at all times while he's in there. I try to reassure him that I can hear him breathe on the monitor and that Babette has a video camera to watch him and that he can make any sort of a noise and we'll come right to him, but that is of no consequence to him and he tells us every day and night.

Each of the last few days my father has asked to sit on the porch in the sun. I throw the ball to Krinkle. We just relax, not really saying much. His pale skin burns in the sun. I spray him with sunblock, put dish towels on his arms, and an XXXL safari hat on his big huge head.

I wonder to myself if he's enjoying his last days in the sun. That he's out here because he doesn't know how many days in the sun he has left. Taking a mental picture before there are no pictures.

My uncle comes by for lunch and sits outside with us on the porch and eats.

"Which is scarier?" he asks my father. "Death or Dying?"

Another long pause. The pauses are so long that sometimes you wonder if he's ignoring you. He looks off away from you. Sometimes down at the floor. I wave my hand in front of him to make sure something bad didn't happen.

"They," Pause. "are," Pause. "two," Pause. "different," Pause. "things." He replies in a raspy weakened voice.

A longer pause.

"Even when you're ready," Pause. "sometimes," Pause. "the body is not."

Another long pause.

"But the journey," Pause. "can be so bad," Pause. "that you welcome death."

My uncle calls the next day before he comes by for a late lunch. "I have someone coming with me today and I think your dad will be excited to see him, but I'm not gonna tell you who it is."

I get my dad out of bed after a nap and clean him up for company. I wheel him out to the living room where my uncle sits on the couch along with another older gentleman with a mustache, a camo baseball cap with a bald eagle and an American flag on it, and two other big fellas. Babette brings up the rear.

My uncle stands as the older gentleman walks steadily over to my dad with a cane. My uncle asks my father, "Blu, do you know who this is?"

My dad looks him over but before he can say anything the gentleman says in a gravelly loud voice, "Bluford! It's Johnny Milliorn!"

My father leans his head back and smiles as big a smile as he could smile. "Well I'll be," he says quietly. He lifts his hand up as far as he can and Johnny reaches out to hold it.

I have heard the name Johnny Milliorn since I was a boy. Johnny grew up on the same street as my dad and Bill. A wild child, I always thought. My father has old black and white photos of Johnny as a kid that he took himself with his camera that we come across every now and again while looking through boxes of photos.

Johnny's two big sons are the two other gentlemen on the couches. He introduces each of them, John and William Bradford.

"I named him after you both!" he says to my Uncle, William (Bill), and my father, Bluford Bradford. The ultimate tribute, I think to myself.

Johnny goes on to tell us about his two other brothers who have both died, and his parents who are also no longer living, and catches us up on his last years. My dad and Johnny had bumped into each other once or twice since high school but it had been years since the last time.

He tells a story about a fight in his driveway between my father and a young bully from school who was harassing Johnny. "You whipped him!" he assures my father.

He reminisces about going to the "picture show" with my dad and my uncle and then playing hide and seek in the old downtown warehouses where my grandfather worked. "I had more fun filthy dirty! God I loved it! I'd like to do it now!" We all laugh imagining them as crazy kids, and my dad loves every minute of it.

For Johnny's grand finale we go out to the driveway to see his '32 Ford kit coupe that he and his son have built. I wheel my father around the car. Johnny opens the doors and shows us the interior complete with air conditioning and power windows. He has a Yosemite Sam painted on the trunk.

We stand in the driveway and Johnny honks as he drives down the street.

It's bright in here. The monitors are beeping in the hall. I can hear the nurses laughing, gossiping to each other. My father is asleep on his uncomfortable, narrow, vinyl bed. We've been in the ER for almost nine hours. They've admitted him overnight after his CT scan said he was impacted with "LOTS of feces" but we've yet to get a room. They'll give him "The Big One" one of my nurse friends tells me, if he needs it. "The Big One" is what they give colonoscopy patients before they cram a robot up their ass or something. The nurse takes photos of my dad's almost pressure sores, I guess so they have proof that they didn't cause them.

My father has been in his bed for three days. His almost pressure sores on his ass from sitting in his wheelchair are so bad he couldn't sit in it at all. He just lay in bed. He hasn't shit in a week and a half. Pressure sores, which are sores that you get on your skin if you remain in one place long enough (in a wheelchair or in a bed for example), we're told are hell, as if my father wasn't in hell already. If you Google them they look like some sort of skin eating virus. Once they start, they're hard to stop. They tell you to put someone on their side to relieve the pain, but my father can't breathe well on his side so I roll him over until it's too much and then I sit him up on his bed. I wedge pillows behind him so he won't topple over. I try to hold his head up. His white beard caked with drool.

I send phone pics of us to my brother and sister. My sister is having her second baby in the morning.

"I love you Dad!" she texts. "You are going to be a grandpa to two little girls tomorrow!"

We finally get a room somewhere near ten o'clock, eleven hours later. They bring in a flat metal rolling box of springs they're swearing is a mattress to the room for me to sleep on. Babette sleeps on a chair. I get possibly the worst sleep of the entire last year, which is an achievement considering the quality of sleep I've gotten in the last year.

They pump my dad full of fluid and he eventually starts going to the bathroom and continues to go to the bathroom on and off for nearly eighteen hours. Nurses come in and out all night like nurses do at hospitals for reasons I can never quite comprehend. My father seems weak, but relatively comfortable all things considered. They weigh him. One hundred fifty-six pounds. That's almost sixty pounds less than when I got home, and he looks it. His mouth hangs open now and his teeth show a bit as if his facial muscles are deteriorating.

I finally get up before the sun rises and sit by the window. I look over downtown El Paso and over into Juarez as the sun comes up, shining peacefully off the windows of the buildings. Eventually I wander out in the hall and pour myself shitty hospital coffee with powdered creamer. Wound care comes by and says they'll get my father another mattress for his sores, but they never bring the mattress.

My sister has her baby, my second niece, Hannah.

"8.6 and healthy," my brother texts with a picture.

I show my father. He smiles a small smile in his hospital bed.

Twelve hours later we finally are released from the hospital. Four hours just waiting to be "checked out."

I ask my dad on the way out, "Are you ok?"

He shakes his head and mouths, "No."

Another month passes. I grow a beard.

We start to look online at tracheotomy tubes. A ventilator is the next and mostly final step in the ALS chapters. The Do Not Resuscitate order in my father's living will trumps sticking a tube in his throat, but as his breathing gets worse I can't blame him for at least looking. We peruse websites. We watch videos of people with "quality lives." One guy went scuba diving. A girl was surrounded by her loving family.

I remember our first trip to the Houston ALS clinic, now years ago. There were representatives from various medical device companies each at tables with brochures and sample devices. We walked from table to table, looking at our future. Not unlike you'd look at a dishwasher or a patio furniture brochure for the home that you're thinking about building. It was surreal. Think I'll get that wheelchair in green, you might say while you're walking, talking, and pointing like a completely normal person with hardly a sign of your disease.

A friend from our support group comes over to talk to us about her experience with a trach. Her husband lived on a trach for five years before he died. I feel guilty wondering if I could possibly live another five years into my forties like this.

She talks to us in detail about what it was like. How it worked. How you suctioned phlegm out of the tube. How her husband used a device to communicate with his eyes until he couldn't control his eyes enough to even use that anymore. He blinked to say yes. Blinked to say no. Then when he couldn't blink anymore, he'd move his eyes to the right for yes and to the left for no. He'd even sleep with his eyes open.

They had decided that when he was completely unable to communicate, they would turn off his ventilator. Somehow her husband was able to muster a "YES" when she asked him if it was time. She takes off her glasses and describes the hospice doctor coming over, sedating her husband, and turning off the vent. He lived for ten or twelve more minutes.

She describes her husband as "happy as a clam," although I have my doubts.

"Would YOU do it again?" I ask her.

"No," she answers bluntly.

She tells us how it was hell. How she didn't sleep for five years.

And I can see my father making the choice not to live so that everyone else might.

Eddie comes by and we roll outside to look at the '41.

"Did you take off the exhaust?" he probes.

"Not yet. I just haven't gotten around to it."

Eddie steps over to the engine. "Put the dipstick in, too. We need to know if it bumps anything on the way in."

I open the rear door and pull the dipstick out from the pile of stuff I've been storing in the car. I look at the pictures on the label. I pull it out of the plastic and hold it up to the transmission. "It goes like this?" I ask, not really knowing.

"You know," Eddie answers, "I'm surprised you didn't pick up on stuff like this over the years."

"Well," I say in my defense, "I am too, but honestly, I don't remember a lot of things like this happening when I was young."

"He never cared," my dad butts in.

I roll my eyes and go back to the dipstick. I frame it up to the transmission the way it looks in the picture, pretending like I'm accomplishing something.

The next day John Attel makes an appearance.

"Let's see that car," he says as he comes in the side door and we all go back out to have a look. John's like the Dalai Lama of car guys. We all have opinions. What we think is the right thing to do. A plan of attack. But we don't do a thing until we get John's blessing.

"Take off the nose," he says right away walking around the car.

I take off the hood and set it by the garage. I look around inside as if I know what I'm looking for. I point and show John where I had cut the crossmember.

Hardly looking, he says, "You might need to do some more cutting," which is code for I'll definitely have to do some more cutting.

"We were worried that maybe it wouldn't go back together right if we took off the nose."

"They weren't together right in the first place."

I walk to the back of the car. "Now what about the rear end?"

A rear end, I did not know, is the same as the rear axle. Of course I always thought the rear end of the car was the actual end of the car on the rear, where you might get rear ended, but this is apparently not so, or maybe it's both, but the rear end everyone talks about in car work seems to be the rear axle.

"Eddie told me to measure from backing plate to backing plate but...I have no idea what the backing plate is." I get down on the ground with a tape measure and crawl underneath the car on the creeper and make John get down with me in his starched work clothes. "This? Or this? Or this?" I point to a few things I think might be the backing plate.

"That one," he says on the third try and gets back up.

I grab the tape measure and measure fifty-five and a half inches.

"Fifty-five and a half inches!" I call out to John from under the car.

John takes out his phone. "Hey! We need a rear end for this '41 that's fifty-five and a half inches. Is that an S-10?" He waits for an answer. "Well, what is it?" He exchanges a few words with his friend

Leon, who owns a junkyard, and hangs up. "He's going to go measure and call me back."

I show him the chrome valve cover I bought on eBay.

"Taiwanese crap?"

"I guess so."

His phone rings.

"A seventy eight Firebird? How much?" He turns toward me. "A seventy eight Firebird. Hundred bucks."

"Well, tell him I want it."

"Alright hold it for us," I can hear Leon on the other end. "Ok bye."

"When he gets it off he'll call me."

"Just let me know when to go get it."

"Alright," John says. "I'm heading back to work. Take that nose off and then we'll see what's next. Bye Uncle Bluie." My dad raises his hand slightly and John reaches to meet it.

My father stays with me by the car after John leaves and I push myself on the creeper to check out the exhaust. The pipe is sticking up into the engine compartment connected to nothing and then on to the muffler and then continues under the car and eventually out the other end.

I text John. "Should I unscrew or cut the exhaust off?"

"Cut the fucker," is the reply, so I get the grinder.

It only takes a few minutes and the front of the exhaust drops to the concrete with a loud clang. The back is mounted to the frame with a bracket and a couple bolts. Once it's off I drag the exhaust out from under the car and place it off to the side of the carport.

I dust off and take stock of what it will take to get the nose of the car off. When I move the body with my hands it doesn't feel too terribly sturdy. You can see that someone had taken off the nose at one point because there are a few mismatched bolts and screws and such here and there. John had told me to take the splash guards off first and then the fenders. The splash guards are the sides of the engine compartment and the fenders are the big round side pieces of the body with the lights on them.

I grab a couple screwdrivers and a few different sized sockets and start with the left splash guard. I unscrew a little here. Unscrew a little there. Some of the bolts come off like they weren't even on, and some of them act like they've been on the car for seventy years. I do the same with the right. Then it's just one bolt after the other. The grill with a fancy "CHEVROLET." The left fender, which I set aside. Then the right fender. And in not too long I'm staring at a car with no front. It doesn't take a math whiz to understand that lining up the engine will be far easier without having to lift it up and into the engine compartment.

My father examines my progress.

"You've done," Pause. "more on this," Pause. "car," Pause. "than I've done," Pause. "in a lifetime."

"You wanna join the circus?"

(inaudible)

"Call the what?"

"EEEEMSTH!"

"AN AMBULANCE?" I shout, completely unsure.

"YETH!" cries my frightened father.

He just started choking out of the blue as I rolled him into his room to take a nap. His petrified eyes are wide open. I straighten his seat and push his heavy torso forward. I stretch and reach for a towel with one hand to wipe the spit from his face and try to keep him upright with the other. I try to confirm that he wants me to call 911. I have never called 911 before. He's gasping for air. His body flailing as much as it can flail. Saliva is everywhere. He can't speak. I wedge my body against his and pull my phone out of my pocket to dial 911.

"Hello, I need an ambulance. My father is choking."

"Is your father breathing?" asks the voice on the other end.

"Yes."

"Is there something in his throat?"

"No. He has ALS. He can't swallow but this is not normal."

We go back and forth with question and answer. The fire station isn't a mile away and while we're talking I hear sirens on my street.

The choking subsides and my father calms down enough to where I can leave him in his room to answer the door. I open the front door and wave to the fire engine slowly moving down my street.

Three firefighters come up the driveway and I bring them into the house and into the living room. I go back and wheel my father to meet them.

They put an oxygen mask on him and ask him questions which I have to answer for him.

I call Babette. She's only a few minutes away.

"Do you want to go to the hospital?" the main firefighter asks my father. He tells me he picked my father up in January, the last time my brother called an ambulance and I was in Jamaica.

My father nods.

"Do you have a DNR?" the second one asks me.

I go to the filing cabinet and search for my father's living will file and his DO NOT RECUSITATE order. I hand it to the firefighter.

An ambulance arrives. Babette walks in the door.

Two EMTs come in the house and put my father on a stretcher and wheel him out to the ambulance. Neighbors have gathered in the driveway. I go to the ambulance door and tell my dad I'll be coming right behind him. I update the neighbors.

Babette rides with my dad in the ambulance and I follow not long after with everything else in the car.

My father is lying in an emergency bed when I arrive. It's a familiar sight, I observe to myself. The doctors go through the routine. They examine him and make sure he's ok to go home, and then we wait to be checked out. It's a short stay.

My brother flies in for our annual motorcycle ride fundraiser down the road in Las Cruces with our support group. It's a fluke of an awful spring day. Windy and cold. Over the last year I've hardly seen my brother, since every time he comes in town I leave.

We only go to the end of the fundraiser to watch the raffle because my dad is too worn out to go to the entire thing. Babette buys seventy-five tickets for the scuba diving prize in hopes that I'll win and can go scuba diving with my brother someday, but I don't win.

We go to dinner after the raffle at a local Italian restaurant. Going to dinner with my father has turned into just a sad affair now since he can neither eat nor drink anything and he can hardly speak to anyone at the table. I move my seat to his side of the table to show him the menu.

"Looks good doesn't it?" I point to a dish.

My father nods and we go through the menu pretending he's going to eat.

The waiter comes by and takes everyone's order.

Babette leans over to my father. "Well, I'm sorry honey, I didn't know you wanted something." She turns to the waiter. "Sir, he would like the special."

We will give the filet to Krinkle and Little Fella.

We stop in the Las Cruces Harbor Freight on the way home. My dad is hell bent on getting a sandblaster. He insists that I need to blast the old grease off the '41 frame before I put the engine in. We'd looked online. We'd asked John Attel.

We buy a soda blaster, which is like a sand blaster but uses baking soda. It's a simple device. There's a large canister where you put the soda and a hose where the soda comes out. You connect your air compressor to it for the pressure. The air comes in, picks up the soda, and pushes it out the hose. The soda "blasts" whatever's in its path.

The only time I've ever seen a sandblaster at work was in junior high school when the maintenance men would sandblast the cholo graffiti off the outside walls of our gym. "FUCK BRANSFORD," our Lincoln Junior High School guidance counselor, it read one morning when we all arrived at school. This thing takes the seventy-year-old grease right off just like the graffiti. My dad sits inside the house looking through a window because the dust is making him choke. In an hour my brother and I have a fair amount of gunk off the frame of the car. We walk into the house to see what my dad thinks of our job.

"You know," he says to both of us. He looks off to the side like he does when he's thinking. He smacks his tongue against the roof of his mouth trying to find moisture. "I know," Pause. "you think," Pause. "I buy too many things." Pause. "But when I," Pause. "buy a hammer," Pause. "I make," Pause. "something," Pause. "for you."

My brother leaves on a Monday but we have tickets booked to San Antonio for the next weekend to pick up a handicap van we bought from a dealership in San Antonio, so we have an excuse to see my sister and her daughters and pass through Austin to see my brother on the way home. We pack the breather, the suction machine, a shower chair, a giant foam wedge so my father can sleep elevated in a hotel, pillows for his head, medicine, and a zillion other things we need for my dad just to get out the door.

But the flying turns out surprisingly to be the smoothest part of the entire trip. Minus one fat bitch complaining to her dipshit boyfriend about our speed checking in on the curb "Isn't it supposed to be fast out here?" every single person in the airport couldn't have been friendlier. Even the curb agent, who usually sticks a hand out for a greedy tip for doing next to nothing, smiles and reassures us that it doesn't matter how long we take to check in. Security takes some time as they go over my dad's chair in detail, but they are nice and we are patient. There's an obnoxious kid next to us giving hell to the TSA agents. He's telling them he's filed a report before with the TSA because "I know the law!". My father and I laugh to ourselves as he's still throwing a fit while they take him into a private room.

Airlines put people who can't walk in an "aisle chair" to get them in a plane. An aisle chair is a straight skinny wheelchair that can fit down the aisle. We wheel down to the gate before the rest of the travelers and I lift my father up and onto the aisle chair which a gate agent has brought to meet us. He straps my father in the chair with criss-crossing seatbelts on his chest and leaves our wheelchair on the ramp to be placed under the plane.

"You might wanna watch his feet," he tells me and I hold my father's feet up a bit off the ground and walk backwards onto the plane guiding my father, the chair, and the gate agent to the first row of seats. We turn the chair around so I can move my dad into a seat. I lift him up and over into an aisle seat and thank the friendly gentleman. We end up moving my dad into the middle seat so Babette and I can take turns holding his head up. He's wearing special underwear that are connected to a bag so he can go to the bathroom without having to use a urinal. We relax. We make a few jokes. Babette gets out her drink tickets so we can have a drink as soon as we're high enough. And for the first time in a very long time, my father looks normal. There is no chair. No breathing machine. No hospital bed. People boarding might not even know he's disabled. Babette and I each order a beer and my father sits back in his chair, closes his eyes, and enjoys the ride.

Our San Antonio hotel has given our roll-in shower room to a "frequent guest" and puts us in merely an "accessible" room with a regular shower until the other is available. An accessible room, although helpful, is nowhere near a substitute for our own home. The bathroom is big enough to turn a wheelchair around in, but aside from that it's mostly just a regular room. It's still hard to open the door, to move through the room, to turn around, to get comfortable, to get my father in and out of bed. We brought the foam wedge with us to try to simulate the raised hospital bed in his bedroom but can't get comfortable and each night we transfer him to his wheelchair to sleep. We move to the room with the roll-in shower but showering proves too difficult so we give up.

My sister comes with her family to introduce us to Hannah, her three-week-old daughter. We sit in the lobby. I chase Emory around the tables and chairs.

We hold Hannah up to my father and rub her little feet against his hands. We put her face up to his lips so he can kiss her, even though he can't pucker his lips anymore.

Dinner proves to be so difficult that I just take my father back to our hotel room and everyone finishes without us.

Our new handicap van is waiting for us at the Ford dealership and we drive the two hours north to Austin to see my brother. We go to Fry's, my father's second favorite store. We watch TV. We sit and look at my brother's giant amazing salt water fish tank.

My brother and I lay a tarp on the bathroom floor so we can bathe my father. My father asks me to get a camera and take a photo in the mirror of the three of us. I hold the camera to my side. We look in the mirror at each other. Me, my brother, and our skin-and-bones father with his shirt off.

A year has passed. An entire year since I came back home. My thirty-sixth birthday has come and gone. Thirty-seven doesn't seem so far away.

My father is enrolled in Hospice. But it isn't like my father is on his death bed and hospice whisks in at the last moment as he breathes his last breath. My father is enrolled in hospice and it's rather uneventful. We sign paperwork and that's pretty much it. But what does change is the care. Immediately, and I mean like the next day, we get bed liners, wipes, first aid cream, a new bed, a better suction machine, you name it. It's like a secret health care key unlocked, well, health care. We have Gabby, our aide who comes to help bathe my father, Linda, our nurse who comes to check on him almost every day, help only a phone call away and without fear or embarrassment. Hospice, it seems, is what being cared for actually should be like. I can't help but think that if we started here, in this way, and cared for the living like hospice cares for the dying, that we might all be better for it.

I remember hospice from when my father's mother died of cancer almost fifteen years before. My grandmother, in stoic Arab fashion, told no one about her breast cancer until we saw the tumor bleeding through her shirt. She was what I would call Christian Scientist with shades of National Enquirer. That is, she never went to the doctor, but she also thought the washing machine could give her cancer. But it had been sixty years since she had been to the hospital and I couldn't find a way to fault that. She lived a simple, meager life with few possessions, one time having her house broken into with the thieves taking...absolutely nothing.

After radiation, she came back to our house, where she had been living already for several years, to a hospital bed in our living room. A nurse came in to sponge bathe her in the bed. She ate less and less. Her body shut down and she eventually lay in a coma. We gave her moisture by wetting a sponge on a straw that she instinctively sucked on. No food, because the organs just didn't need nourishment anymore. It was as if you come in as you go out. Helpless. Like a baby.

"Your grandmother is gone," my father told us early one morning knocking on our bedroom doors. We had all come home from Austin in anticipation of her dying. We walked to the living room. It was the first time I had ever seen a dead body.

I fly to Vegas for a friend's wedding. I catch a 7pm flight, change into a tux, go to the Viva Las Vegas Wedding Chapel, hit the tables, lose a hundred bucks, go to bed at 4am, and am in a cab at 6am to catch a flight home in time to run into Eddie in the driveway looking at the engine mounts.

"Blu Two!" he greets me.

"Hi Eddie. I'm just coming from the airport." I shake his hand.

I put my things inside and come back out to the car. "Can we line up the mounts? 'Cause I'm really not sure how they fit."

"Of course," Eddie says and I grab the pile of brackets from the box along with the instructions, which I hand to Eddie. He eyes them for a moment but already knows which way they fit. He picks up a piece of the mount and holds it up to one side of the engine. "These go here on this side, and the other," he points to the pile of stuff on the ground, "go on the other side."

"And these," he takes a different part and walks over to the '41 "go here." He places the other half of the mount squarely over the frame of the car. Then the two will marry together with a rubber spacer and a big long bolt. The instructions say to measure seventeen inches from a particular hole in the frame and put the center of the left mount at that spot. We measure and set the bracket on the frame. Eddie gives it a once over and says, "Yeah, that looks about right."

As is his M.O., he doesn't stay long and simply tells me to call him after I have the engine mounted.

I grab my father and wheel him out to watch me take a stab at the engine.

My sockets are lying on the ground where I seem to be leaving them. I know my dad hates this. The engine mounts have only three bolts apiece to put in so it doesn't take much time to get those pieces attached to the engine. As I get them tight I look over to my father who nods in approval.

I pump up the cherry picker until the engine and the transmission lift off the ground and then give it sorta small but forceful pushes. Cherry pickers don't move smoothly. It kinda goes a little left and then you move it back right. Then it goes right and you move it back left. Then it gets stuck on something like a small stick on the ground and you have to sweep in front of it and start again. The engine starts to swing heavily on the chain. Eventually you get it where you want it.

It takes a bit of pushing and lowering and pulling and raising to get the engine and transmission into the engine compartment. Attaching the mounts on the engine to the brackets on the frame is a bit more tedious, but after trial and error I manage to get everything bolted together and from what I can tell everything looks like it's where it's supposed to be.

I get a floor jack to support the transmission that has yet to be attached to the crossmember, and take my dad inside.

The next day I go to see Leon about the Firebird rear end. Dyer Auto Salvage is about as far as you can go over the mountain and out into the northeast side of town. Any further and you run into the White Sands Missile Range and eventually the New Mexico mountains.

I love the way the junkyard is organized by parts. Like a library of junk. When you walk in the gate, there are rows of wheels on old wooden shelves to the right. To the left is a table of shocks. Every so often there's a transmission on the ground.

The office is as crammed as the yard. Small parts hanging on the walls. Parts on the counter. It smells of grease. I nod to Leon as I walk in and wait for another customer to finish up.

I introduce myself and he shakes my hand over the counter. "How's your dad?" he asks me. Leon knows my family. He looks like he could be related to Babette's family with his olive skin and thick goatee.

"Well, he's hanging in there," I spare him the details.

"What did you say that rear measured?"

"Fifty-five and a half inches backing plate to backing plate. I think you said there was a Firebird rear that matched." I throw backing plate in like I always knew what a backing plate was.

Leon puts a walkie-talkie from the counter to his mouth. "Big Ray!" he calls into it.

"Yeah!" Big Ray responds from somewhere out in the yard.

"Can you get me the '78 Firebird rear? I've got someone here who wants to take a look at it. And measure a couple others. We're looking for fifty-five and a half."

"Ok!" Big Ray says into the staticky walkie-talkie.

Leon turns to me. "Are you gonna use the old leaf springs?"

"Well...I guess so," I say timidly, since I really don't know what a leaf spring is.

"I would. Just put the rear right on the old leafs. You just want this thing to drive, right?"

"Just down the street."

"Then definitely use the springs. They'll be fine," Leon says and I nod like I know what he's talking about.

He picks up the walkie-talkie again. "Big Ray! I'm sending him out to you to have a look."

"Ok!" Big Ray answers back.

"Go out the gate there," Leon points out the office window. "Go to the left and you'll see Big Ray by the building on the other side of the yard. He'll show you the rears."

I walk through the parts library, open the gate, and walk into the proper junkyard. Cars forever. Hoods up. Jacked up. Wheels missing. Exactly what you think of when you think of a junkyard. I can see Big Ray on his way to meet me.

Big Ray is about 6'2", 275, with an absolutely enormous bald head, a thick neck to meet it, and a big baby face. He is covered in sweat and grease.

I reach out my hand, "Hey Big Ray. I'm Blu."

"Hey. Big Ray. Over this way," he nods back behind him.

I follow him to the racks of rear axles on the far side of the junkyard. While we're walking I ask, "Hey, can you tell me what a leaf spring is? Are they the curved things under the car that the wheels sit in? I'm a bit of a novice here."

He points under a car next to the axles. "Exactly. You can see one right there."

"Ah ok. That's what I thought," And I really did think it.

Big Ray shows me the pile of rear ends. He shows me the Firebird rear and we measure it again to confirm the size. We measure several others, but the Firebird fits. He radios to Leon. "Ok I'm sending him back in. I'll get it ready."

I walk back across the yard and into the office and chat with Leon for a bit. He tells me to drive around to the back gate and Big Ray will bring the rear end to me there. I pay him a hundred bucks and thank him.

Big Ray meets me with a forklift at the back gate and puts the rear end in my truck. I thank him too and drive back home with a big heavy piece of my puzzle.

Carlos calls looking for work.

"Hola Blu, Te habla Carlos."

"Andale Carlos! Necessito ayuda con mi carro hoy. Possible tres or cuatro horas mas o menos," I try in my best present tense Spanish to tell him I need a few hours of car help.

"Bueno, ahorita ya me voy." *I'll be right over.*

"Ok adios."

I had the idea that I would make an attempt at bolting in the engine and transmission mounts myself, but I need to do some welding and frankly my welding skills fall somewhere between "lucky" and "suck" and Carlos is a great welder. I put my work boots on and Carlos must have been around the corner because he is in the driveway when I get downstairs.

"Buenos días!" I call, walking out the door.

"Buenos días!" Carlos answers back.

I meet him at the gate and we walk over to the car.

"Necessito poner tornillos en los soportes al lado del motor y abajo del transmission entonces soldar los soportes." *I need to bolt and weld the motor mounts and the transmission mounts.* I open the door, reach into the back seat of the '41, and hand the diagrams that came with the mounting kits to Carlos.

"Mira." *Look here.*

Everything is already in temporary place. I have the mounts on the engine but they need to be bolted to the frame and then welded for safe measure. I have the crossmember bolted to the transmission and clamped to the frame, but also that needs to be welded together and then bolted to the frame. The instructions look simple. Cut the crossmember to size, weld it to the supports, clamp the thing in place, drill the holes and bolt to the frame.

We lie on our backs and wiggle under the car to have a look. I point here and there to show Carlos what I have set up.

"Mira. Yo pon...eh? Pon...i?"

"Puce," Carlos corrects. *I put.* An irregular verb.

"Ok. Yo puce los supportes aquí," I point to the middle of the transmission where the two main support bolts connect to the transmission, "pero necessitamos connect..."

"Connectados," he corrects again.

"Necesitamos connectados con los tornillos. Pero primero necesitamos soldar el tubo en este bracket," I stumble to a Spanglish finish. It's the tenses that are the hardest. You can speak everything in the present. "I do this tomorrow." "I do this yesterday." But to have a reasonable conversation you gotta know the tenses.

Carlos gives everything a look and gets a quick handle on what we need to do.

"Puntos aquí, y puntos aquí," he points to where we need to tack weld the cross bar to the brackets. Tack welding is where you just zap a weld in a dot to keep something in place but then finish the complete weld later. We need to tack weld the bar to the brackets that are clamped to the frame, drill holes for the bolts, and then take the whole thing off and weld it solid to the brackets. Then put it back on the frame, bolt it back to the transmission and then bolt the brackets to the frame.

I wheel the welder out to the car and hand Carlos a mask and welding gloves. I put my own mask on and Carlos zaps a couple tack welds.

"Quieres probarlo?" He pokes his head up and holds the torch up towards me. *Do you want to try it?*

"Sí sí," and we swap places and he gives me the gloves.

"Aquí y aquí y aquí," he shows me where to weld.

I tack the crossbar to the brackets.

I grab an electric drill. An electric drill because you just don't get the power you need with a battery drill, my dad had told me. I let Carlos have at the bolt holes. Drilling holes through thick metal isn't exactly easy. Like plenty of manual labor, it's not the science behind it, it's the actual work involved. You lie on your back. You punch a tiny mark with a hammer in the metal so your drill bit doesn't walk all over the place when you start to drill. You squeeze a drill in between the ground and the car frame. And then you push up into the frame with your drill as hard as you can while the bit slowly shaves away a hole. You spit out the metal shavings. You get some in your eye. And you do it twice. Once with a smaller drill bit to get the hole started, and then again with a bigger bit to make the hole the right size. And then you do it twenty-three more times to get every bolt bolted.

We move to the other side of the car and do the same thing. Babette wheels my dad outside to watch.

After the bar is tacked and the holes are drilled we unclamp everything and take the crossmember to the welding table to weld it solid to the brackets. Carlos takes the lead, of course, offering me a couple of spots to practice. When the bar is solid we go back to the car to bolt everything into place.

Carlos does the dirty work and then also welds the sides of the brackets to the frame for a little extra security. I put the bolts in place.

We blow the dust off of ourselves with the compressor hose and I tell Carlos to call me soon because I'll probably need him again. We shake hands. I pay and thank him.

I walk over to the '41 and lie down on the creeper and roll under the car to take a look. I reach up and grab the crossmember and pull on it just to make sure it's solid. The engine and transmission are finally where they need to be.

It turns out there's not much to removing the rear end of a car. I had already accidentally severed the emergency brake cables from the back wheels when I cut out the original crossmember from the frame. The original brake lines had also snapped off the rear end from just being too old. And the old shocks are just dangling from the frame unattached to the rear end for who knows why. Nothing is really keeping the rear end to the rest of the car except the u-bolts. To remove a rear end all you really have to do is unbolt the four u-bolts holding the axle to the leaf springs. So I jack up the car, put the rear end on jack stands and take off the two rear tires. Then I take the u-bolts off with the impact wrench. After the u-bolts are off, the rear end just lifts off. It's surprising how easily it comes off. I have to do some maneuvering to get it out from under the car as it's still connected to the drive shaft, but before long I'm pulling the old rear end out from under the car and pushing it over to the side of the carport.

Installing the new rear end is basically doing the exact opposite. Lifting up is harder than letting down but I have some help from my cousin who happens by on his bike, so with a pair of extra hands we lift one side of the rear up and over the right leaf spring and then push it out to the side of the car to bring the other side in. Then we lift that up and push the axle back so that the other side will push through and rest on the left leaf spring. And that's it. The rear end hangs on the springs, ready to be bolted in.

The old u-bolts, like a lot of the old stuff, won't fit on the new rear end, so I call Leon to see if he has anything at the junkyard. I measure what I think are the dimensions and he says he'll have a look and call me if he finds something. He calls the next day and says he had some bolts from a Suburban that will probably work, so my dad and I go over the mountain and out to the edge of town to go get them.

I wheel my dad up to the door so Leon can say hello, but the door is too small to get the chair inside so we just stay outside.

Leon is carrying the bolts and plates in his arms. The plates are a flat piece of metal that the bolts bolt through and then sort of cinch up against the rear end. "They're big bolts but they measure right and have the plates with them," Leon says.

My dad grunts to get my attention. "Breather."

I take my father back out to the van where I set him up facing the gate with his BIPAP machine plugged into the cigarette lighter and stretched out of the passenger door so he can see me just inside the yard. He just can't make it very long without the breathing machine anymore. It seems like every day he needs it more. I go back into the office, but keep poking my head out and yelling to my dad with a thumbs up to make sure he's ok. He nods to let me know.

"What are you gonna do for shocks?" Leon asks me.

"Well, I guess I don't know what I'm gonna do," I say, totally unsure.

"You should just put regular shocks on it. That's what I'd do. Those knee-action shocks aren't worth keeping." Knee-action shocks. That's a new one but makes sense if you saw what the shocks look like.

We walk outside the office door and he points to the bed of shocks against the office wall. "Just put a simple shock on the rear end. Mount it to the frame. It's easy."

I walk over to the shocks and pick a white one up. "Alright, well, then I can do that," I say, not really knowing anything about shocks, or that I had to put any in, or how in the heck to put them in. Everyone always says everything is easy.

"Hey, you still got that Kharmann Ghia?" he asks. "I know someone who will buy it from you."

"Still got it, but I think my dad would sooner give it to someone than sell it. I don't think it's going anywhere but I can call you if he changes his mind." I pay twenty dollars for the bolts and plates.

Leon comes out to the van to say goodbye to my father. "Take your dad that way," he points west towards nowhere. "You wouldn't believe it Blu," he says to my father. "There are two thousand houses now out there." He looks back at me. "Go show your dad before you go home."

We watch YouTube videos that night of people replacing shocks. The good news is that there doesn't seem to be a tried and true method for mounting shocks. Some people do it beautifully and some people do it like Frankenstein, and since I'm likely to fall into the latter I'm feeling pretty good about what it's going to take to get some new shocks on the old car.

"It gets worse," my dad croaks. His head barely visible above the yellow blanket wrapped up to his neck and his breathing mask covering most of the rest of his face.

"What gets worse?" I lean in to him to try and read his lips.

"Every moment," Pause. "of my life," he scratchily finishes.

I grab the towel that we keep on his bed and wipe the saliva from his mouth. "Shit Dad," I say, and pull a chair up to his bed.

"I think of death," Pause. "like it's the," Pause. "same thing I was," Pause. "doing ten months before," Pause. "I was forced."

"Before you were forced? Say it again. Ten months before what?" It's so hard to interpret.

"I was," Pause. "ever," Pause. "conceived."

"Conceived. Ok. Before you were BORN," I explain it out loud to myself. "So one month before nine."

"That's the way," Pause. "I look at it."

"You're saying it's no different between before you existed and when you don't after you die?"

"Exactly."

"I don't know," I say and I don't. "I mean, I guess it would stand to reason if there was nothing after then there was nothing before. Or vice versa. I mean, I don't know."

Silence.

I continue. "It's a weird thing to think about. It's the thing that confuses me the most about existing. Eternity. Suppose you didn't exist at all. I mean, I guess it doesn't matter. You're not gonna know.

176

Eventually it's not gonna matter to us. It's not gonna matter to anybody. But still to think that things go on eternally, forever, is so bizarre to me. I can't quite mentally come to terms with it. I can think of the year 4500 but still that's not even close. That's 2500 years away. That's nothing compared to how far back or how far forward it goes. And it still doesn't account for the present, and cognition, and awareness, and this. And not that there has to be some sort of powerful meaning attached to this conversation even though it's important in the context of our universe, but still the fact that this moment exists is still totally unexplained. I mean, suppose it's lights out for eternity. That's fine. But that still doesn't account for it. It still doesn't explain one single solitary thing about being here. Even if it's totally meaningless, it still doesn't say why."

My dad's heavy breathing fills the room.

I go on. "And if we evolved, then it makes us even less important. The fact that we grew from some lesser being, from some reptile that grew legs and crawled out of the water up on to the land, makes this moment even less meaningful. It makes it only a process of development. The fact that we live in a house with refrigerated air is just a point in the process. But it still doesn't say anything about, I mean, forget us, just consider the sun and the moon and the planets. It explains nothing. There can't just be a non-answer can there? A non-answer is not really an answer for me."

My dad waits.

"Tinkle," he whispers.

"Oh."

Because in the search for the meaning of life, I guess you still have to pee.

Shocks, fundamentally, are pretty simple. They add support to your vehicle. Make your bounce less bouncy. You attach one end to the axle and the other to the frame.

I remove the older knee action shocks because everyone seems to tell me I need to, but mostly because they don't line up anymore with the new rear end. Removing them is easy and the shocks leave a nice long hole in the frame that looks to me like I can shove a big long bolt back through and I'll have the upper bolt to mount the top of the new shock.

Eddie startles me at the door.

"Blu Two!" he says through the door window.

I open the door and shake his hand. "You're just the person I need to see! Lemme grab my dad." I walk away and come back with my dad in his wheelchair.

"Mister Blu. How are you?" Eddie reaches out and touches my father's hand.

My father shrugs and raises his eyebrows in a sorta "Well, I'm here," and mouths an "Ok," but doesn't really speak.

We all go outside.

"Some progress I see," Eddie says as he looks around the car.

I point to the rear of the '41, "I need to put on some shocks. I took the old knee action shocks off and here's what I'm thinking," I grab a bolt from the ground and hold it up to the bottom of the axle. "Bottom attaches here," I point down to the shock plate. "And then putting a bolt through up here," I point to the hole from the old shock. "Does that look like that'll work?"

Eddie answers with a story.

"A civil engineer named Carl Huddle taught me to fly. He loved to fly so he started a flying club so he could afford to fly. Around Christmas we went to Lubbock to pick up his two kids. Beautiful weather when we left El Paso. We fly out to Lubbock, pack them up and fly on back. As we're coming up on El Paso International, I'm flying, the kids are asleep and Carl's just looking out the window. I'm listening to the tower and they start to speak of these terrible crosswinds. The numbers they were giving me I knew exceeded the physical capability of the airplane. I line up on the runway about thirty miles from the airport and I start to press down on the rudder. More rudder. More rudder. And when I realized I've used up all the rudder and I had the aircraft perpendicular to the runway I turned to Carl and said, "Carl I'm in trouble here, I've used up all the rudder." And Carl just kept looking out the window. I knew if I let up any pressure on the rudder the wind was just gonna blow me away and I was already going slow enough to land that I was probably going to crash. But when I almost saw the wingtip touch the runway, I took my foot off the rudder and just kind of dropped the plane on to the runway and it bounced around and screeched.

When we got down to the general aviation area and took the kids and luggage off, in kind of a calm subdued rage I said "Carl! I was in trouble up there and I asked you, I used up the rudder what do I need to do?"

And he said, "You do everything it takes to land the airplane."

We drive to just outside of Dallas for the Fourth of July, for what I figure might be one of my father's last trips anywhere. Traveling, even in our new van, is just not what it used to be. Being almost anywhere but home has suddenly, or maybe not so suddenly, become difficult and uncomfortable for my father. But we have a fun, meaty holiday BBQ party at my father's cousin's house on Cedar Creek Lake. My father sits on the boat dock in his wheelchair and watches us jump in the water. We watch fighter planes in the sky from a distant air show. There are fireworks lighting up the lake as far as we can see. My sister and her daughters drive up from Austin with my brother. I have scanned about three hundred old photographs for everyone to look at. We gather around the dining room table and have a grand time listening to all the cousins talk about being young. My sister cries seeing photos of my father as a baby, lying on a blanket in the grass in Paris, Texas.

We drive with my brother to Austin for a few days and then make the long drive back home across Texas. I watch my father in the rearview mirror. For six hundred miles he looks out the left window of the van because he can't turn his head enough anymore to look forward. His mouth hangs open. I can see his teeth like a skeleton. He drools onto a washcloth we placed on his shoulder. In the rearview he looks at me with his eyes and then looks up to the roof and mouths "UP!" telling me to turn up the radio when a Chuck Berry song comes on. We drive in more or less a straight line from central to west Texas.

Madeline Stevens dies in what seems to me like out of the blue. She had contracted pneumonia and passed away in the hospital like many ALS patients do. She was diagnosed with bulbar onset ALS not a year or two before. We didn't know Madeline well since it was a rapid decline in the year after we met, and we only saw her and her family once a month at group meetings, but more than that, the bulbar onset had taken her voice almost immediately. She couldn't speak to us. She carried a handkerchief to wipe the drool from her mouth and when she was unable to do that on her own her husband did it for her. She moved slowly and used a walker more and more each meeting. She and her family would arrive and leave early, and that's all we really knew of Madeline.

We follow the Franklin Mountains to Las Cruces for the service. Babette walks ahead and I wheel my father into the funeral home. We stop and say hello to Madeline's daughter. She thanks us for coming. We wave to a few people from our group, but for the most part don't really know anyone at the funeral. The chaplain gives a friendly and light-hearted eulogy. He opens the mic to the room, and people get up to say a few words.

We learn that not only did Madeline have a voice, but her life *was* her voice. She was a drug and alcohol counselor and a former addict herself. She helped her husband recover. She healed. She saved. One by one people approached the podium and told stories of how they'd be dead if it weren't for Madeline's words. She literally talked them into living.

And it dawns on me that we really don't know much about anyone in our group other than their suffering. We love going to Madeline's service because we get to learn about her. And in a sad way, it's the only way we'll ever get to learn about anyone with ALS. Someone will have to *tell* us who they were before the disease.

I wish that they knew my dad. I wish that they knew what a great lawyer he was. How much he loved his children. How good of a builder he was. How he would never let you buy dinner. How he could often barely tell a funny story because he would laugh so hard before he even got the words out. But they will never know that, I guess, until he dies and has a service of his own.

"Back," my dad says and points his chin towards the back door.

"You wanna go outside?"

"Yes," he nods.

"Ok. Like all the way to the back?"

"Yes!" His eyes open wide like it's a stupid question.

That's the way every conversation seems to go these days. Now, my dad has always sorta done whatever it is that he's gonna do. That's just his style. When he could speak a little better and you asked him a question about something he needed you to do for him, his answer was almost always, "First, because I want to. And second," some other reason, if he even offered one, as if he needed a better reason. But more because I think he felt like somehow you were trying to stop him from doing whatever it was that he wanted to do and since he couldn't do it himself maybe he felt threatened. But you weren't asking to try to stop him, you were just asking to ask him, like anyone asks anyone anything. At least that's what you thought you were doing. But that's never the way he sees it, and it probably wasn't the way you asked it if you were being honest with yourself. And so now that he can't really talk it's morphed into him telling you what he wants you to do step by step, but he never tells you two steps in advance. He tells you one step at a time, and you can't ask him what the next step is. You just have to do the first step, and then the second, and on and on until you've done what he wants to do. Clever and simple enough, but like many things seem to do these days, has unfortunately on several occasions ended in a screaming blow out with me yelling something along the lines of "NORMAL FUCKING PEOPLE HAVE CONVERSATIONS!" or "WHY IN THE FUCK

WON'T YOU TALK TO ME?!" and then my father telling me to be quiet or not to start my shit again.

His frustration is obvious. It's hard for him to talk. It takes energy and exhausts him. He doesn't like to repeat things. He shakes his head "NO!" when you don't get the words. "It doesn't matter" he says. "Yes it DOES matter!" I say back to him. "NO!" he says again and then I throw something and storm ten feet away to my computer or to the bathroom or nowhere really because there isn't anywhere to really storm off to.

In this case the first step is "back" so I wheel him out the back door and into the yard and bounce him all the way to the back of the backyard to the gigantic piles of scrap wood that we have accumulated for years behind the back garage.

I turn him to face the piles. He points with his eyes to the bottom of the shelves we had Willie build a while back to store the wood lengthwise. There's some PVC pipe on the ground.

"This?" I point and walk over to the PVC.

My father shakes his head.

"This?" I point to something else near where I think he's looking.

He shakes his head again with a look I could swear is a "No, stupid" but probably isn't.

I point to an old metal rod.

"This?" Surely not.

"YES!" he nods in a big long nod like it's completely obvious to everyone in the world except for me that he's looking for an old metal rod on the bottom of the wood pile.

"What is it?" I look back at him.

"Closet," he says. It's an old closet rod that used to be in the house.

I move a few pieces of wood around to loosen up the rod and pull it out and stand it on its end. It's at least seven feet long.

He looks with his eyes in the direction of the house.

"Back inside?"

He shakes his head. Not inside.

"The front?" I guess.

"Yes," he nods.

"The car?" I guess again.

"YES," he nods even stronger.

"Well, shit Dad, I have no idea what you're talking about."

I wheel him back through the yard and around the house to the '41 carrying the rod at my side.

Step two.

I pull him up beside the car. "Ok. Now what?"

"Bolt," he says, which I guess means to pick up one of the long bolts lying on the ground that I had bought to use as the top mount for my shock. I set the closet rod down and grab the bolt off the ground and hold it up so he can see it.

"Cut that," and he looks with his eyes to the rod. "as a spacer," Pause. "on the inside," he looks back at the bolt, "for that."

Step three.

I look at the rod and back to the bolt and wrap my hand around the bolt like it's the closet rod trying to understand what he's talking about. I grab a bolt and put it through the frame and get down on the ground and under the car. I put my hand around the bolt and look at it again.

"Aaah haa!" I say out loud and shimmy to stick my head out from under the car. "So the shock hits the rod and the rod hits the frame and that stops the bolt from coming back out of the frame."

He nods the biggest nod of all. "EXACTLY!" it reads.

If I believed things happen for a reason, which I do not, it's almost as if maybe the rod had been sitting there waiting all this time just so it could be found again by me in the backyard years later so it could be used as a spacer for a bolt on the frame as the upper shock mount on the '41.

The next day while my father's sleeping I get out the chop saw and have a crack at the shocks. A chop saw looks like any circular saw really except it's spring loaded and you sorta use a chop motion as you bring the blade down onto whatever you're cutting. If you're cutting metal it showers a bunch of sparks in the air and slowly cuts as you press down. It cuts a piece of metal in half with not that much effort at all. I measure what I think I need to cut out of the closet rod and cut two pieces about two inches long each.

I shove the bolts, shocks, washers, and nuts under the car, and roll under the body on the creeper to put everything together. Assembling takes some strength, some massaging, and a little bit of time but comes together mostly like I think it's gonna come together, and actually looks pretty darn clean, closet rod and all.

John Attel had dropped off some wheels for me to use temporarily until I bought some new ones, so I put those on and lower the car down to have a look. I take a photo with my phone and send it to John.

"Well, that ain't right," he sends back to me.

The tires are butted up against the front of the fenders. "Yeah. I didn't think so."

John comes by after work and has a look. There's a button of sorts on the bottom of a leaf spring that fits in a hole on the shock plate and keeps the rear end centered on the springs. John figures out that the hole on the old rear end's shock plates is set further forward than the new plates for some reason, so to center the wheels I'll have to take my shocks apart and remove the shock plates and drill new holes as far forward on the plate as I can, and then reassemble the shocks and see if that will push the wheels back a couple more inches towards the rear.

I take them apart. My dad supervises, Babette holds the plates in place on the drill press, and I do a relatively kludgey job of measuring and drilling new holes. Then I sit down and file them by hand until the bolts on the leaf springs pop back into place. I put the shocks back together just like I had before, drop the car back down to the ground, and sure enough get two or three more inches out of the wheels. Things look right. The shocks are done.

My dad and I look online for a gas tank. I figure the old one has to be rusted out or not usable (not because I know of course, but just because I think it), and really I haven't looked to see if there even is a gas tank under the car. John says they should cost a couple hundred bucks and we find one that looks about right. But before I buy it I want to get the old one out, so my dad and I roll outside and I crawl under the car. There is indeed a gas tank, and it does look a little rusty on the bottom. The tank should be secured to the frame with metal straps, but I look from side to side and don't see any straps.

"I'm looking for some straps on this thing but I don't see any!" I call out to my dad from under the car. I look a bit more and push myself out into daylight.

"I don't see any straps, Dad. All I see is one bolt on the lip of the tank on this side," I point to the right side, "and two on the other side. But no straps."

My dad shrugs.

So we go back inside and we look again online. I ask my neighbor Doug who leaves a copy of instructions in my mailbox on how to remove a gas tank on a '41 Chevy that he found on the Internet. It says to remove the straps and it'll come right off. I go back out under the car and I still don't see straps. I join a Chevy online forum and post in a thread that I'm trying to take a gas tank out of a '41 and several people reply that all I have to do is take the straps off. But I still don't see any straps. I sit with my dad again at the computer looking for how in the world I get a gas tank out of my car and really the one in the picture doesn't even look like my gas tank.

So just for the heck of it I look up a 1940 Chevy tank.

I turn and look at my dad. "I think I figured it out."

"Well, what is it?" he says to me silently with his raised eyebrows.

"I think the '41 is a '40."

And it was. A '40 after all these years. Born a '40. Lived a '40. Stored a '40. Ignored a '40. But named a '41. And that's the way we decide to keep it.

I wheel my dad outside and I crawl under the car for the howevermanyth time to turn the rusty bolts on the gas tank. One of them is so rusty and tight that I stick my legs out from under the car and use my feet against the brick wall to push. It takes some good pushing and pulling to dislodge the filler tube—the tube that goes from the gas tank to where you stick a gas pump, but unscrewing the gas line is simple and the tank just drops right down into my hands and I place it on the ground. I roll out from under the car and my dad and I take stock. The tank smells of, well, gas, which surprises me actually since it has been sitting unused for decades, but it actually looks to be in pretty good shape on the top and sides and really only has a little rust on the bottom.

I call John Attel to ask him about the tank. "What should I do with it?"

"Take the sending unit off and look inside the thing."

"Ok…and what's the sending unit?"

"It's the only thing on there that you can take off."

"Just look in it with a flashlight or something?"

"A match."

I take off the sending unit (five small screws) which I learn is the "unit" that "sends" the level of the gas tank to the gas gauge. There's a little floating piece of cork attached to the "unit" and depending on where the cork is it "sends" a reading through a wire to the gauge which tells you how much gas you have in the tank.

"What's next?" I text.

"Drive shaft."

John calls Leon and Leon brings a yoke home with him from his junkyard. John leaves it on my front porch before I wake up one morning.

I Google "yoke" to see what in the heck a yoke is.

I call Leon at the junkyard and ask him if he thinks I should get a used driveshaft and cut it (because Eddie Solis had told me that's what you have to do to a used drive shaft usually) or get a new one.

"You're telling me that you had me take a yoke off a driveshaft to give you the yoke and you needed a driveshaft too?"

A yoke, I learn, is the piece that connects the transmission to the driveshaft. It slides into the end of the transmission and has to be disassembled to remove it. It's possible that he could have just given me an entire driveshaft, yoke included.

"Well, I guess so, but I'm just following orders here," I deflect, and really have no idea what it took to get a yoke off a driveshaft or at the time that a yoke was attached to the driveshaft to begin with.

"If it were me," he says, "I'd get a new one. Couple hundred bucks and it'll look good and clean."

A sigh of relief.

"Where do I get one?"

"Only one place in town," he says. "U-Joints Incorporated."

I look up U-Joints, give them a call, and tell them what I need. They tell me to bring my yoke in and they'll show me exactly how to measure for the driveshaft. I print and take a photo of the differential so they can see what the other end looks like and point me to where I need to measure. The differential is the pumpkin-looking thing on the rear end where the rear end of the driveshaft connects.

I put my dad in the van and we drive to the other side of town, or what used to be the other side of town but is now practically the center of town. U-Joints is on a street of warehouses. Other car places. Industrial-type business. I park and put our portable ramp on the sidewalk, because sometimes old buildings aren't handicap accessible, and wheel my dad up and inside.

I show a man at the counter the yoke and my picture, and after a bit of consulting with two other guys in the shop he points to the center of one side of the ring on the yoke, and the flat surface on what he called the pinion yoke on the rear differential. There are apparently yokes on both sides of the driveshaft.

"Put the yoke all the way in the transmission. Then pull it out about an inch and measure from there. Center to center," he calls it. "And make sure your car is on the ground." Both Eddie and John had told me this, but seeing it in front of me makes actual sense to me.

My dad and I go back home to measure.

"Forty-seven inches!" I call out to my dad and scoot out from under the car. "Forty-seven inches."

My father and I take the yoke and the measurement back to U-Joints and by the end of the week have a new shiny black driveshaft in our hands.

It's August. The Eli Young Band puts out another record with two of my songs on it. A verse from "My Old Man's Son" reads:

> From the way I laugh
>
> To the way I hold a woman's hand
>
> Everywhere I go wherever I run
>
> I'll be my old man's son

I call my father an asshole. Or more specifically, I tell him he's an asshole to everyone, which may have been a bit of an exaggeration. For the second time in a month Babette asks me if I want to leave, and that she doesn't know what she'll do but that there's too much fighting and it has to stop. And she's right, but my father can be so mean, I think selfishly, even when he doesn't say a word. He has a brutal stare. Like a visual death punch.

I often tell people how calm he is. If you knew my father way back when, you'd know he had a bit of a temper and was intimidating as fuck. You wouldn't even consider messing with him. Not because he was big and strong, though he was, but because he could shut you down with a couple words. And if you happened to be on the receiving end of a blow by my father, which only happened one time that I ever saw and that was after a soccer coach punched him in the face at a soccer game as they were arguing about a call on the field, you'd wish it was only a sentence. My father was a bad motherfucker, and somehow he was still a bad motherfucker.

But now he's like a Zen bad motherfucker. He doesn't move. He doesn't talk. He doesn't even get mad. He's accepted his condition in a way that I never thought possible. In a way that I could never do. But he is still very capable of bringing you to your knees just by looking at you.

When my grandmother died, she gave my father a hundred thousand dollars. It was the only money my father ever really had. He spent every single penny he ever made in his life. He had no savings account. No retirement. He bought things he wanted when he had money to buy them. He had a home, a car, and tools to rival Home Depot, but not too much else.

In the late nineties I was working tech jobs in Austin. I made a lot of money for a twenty-three year old, I thought. I put some money away. Had a broker. My dad gave me his mother's money to invest for him, so like everyone did in the late nineties, I put it into tech stocks. And like everyone did, we lost our asses when the tech bubble burst. But we weren't trying to make a million dollars or anything. We were just trying to invest our money like everyone tells you to do. But they don't tell you about the people that rig the game. They don't tell you that when they get out with their piece and the game folds you'll be stuck with nothing and you'll never catch up. They tell you to do it again. And you do. And you do it again. And again.

The stocks eventually made their way back up to where they were originally years later, before they took another beat down by the housing bubble. And then another with the recession. My father bought his van, gave my brother some money for a down payment on a truck. And his one hundred dwindled down to ten after a forty percent loss.

And so one day my dad decides he wants to buy another car. A thirty-five thousand dollar car. And I tell him he doesn't have thirty-five thousand dollars to buy a car.

And he throws me a visual death punch. A "What the fuck are you talking about I don't have thirty-five thousand dollars of my own fucking money in the bank and what the fuck did you do with it you better fucking tell me right the fuck now," kinda punch. He stares at me like I burned the money.

"What the hell do you think I did with your money, Dad? What do you think I spent it on?"

Stare.

"Look, you can be angry that the money's gone, but I'm no thief."

STARE.

"I DID NOT STEAL YOUR GODDAMN MONEY!"

STARE.

"YOU CAN HAVE EVERY PENNY I HAVE IN THE BANK! TAKE IT! I DON'T FUCKING WANT IT! THERE IS TWENTY-FIVE THOUSAND DOLLARS IN AN IRA THAT I PUT THERE FIFTEEN YEARS AGO! TAKE THE MONEY AND BUY YOUR STUPID GODDAMN CAR THAT YOU DON'T NEED!"

STARE.

I throw something. I storm off up the stairs. I pout on the bed.

But of course I mean it. He can have my money. Hell, he deserves the money. But the real truth of it probably is, that when you save money, you don't expect to die. You expect to live. You expect to have time for your money to grow, or bounce back, or do something. But when you're dying I guess there is no bounce back. There is only now.

Several weeks later while watching a movie my dad turns to me and says, "I want that twenty-five thousand dollars."

I walk out of the room.

I was laid off in January 2001 from my tech job, as were most people at tech companies around then. I had been the seventh person hired on our way to three hundred at our peak. We raised a hundred and forty million dollars in an IPO, made a Super Bowl commercial, and overdid it like everyone overdid it. In our defense, we actually manufactured a device that was a bit before its time, in my opinion, which fifty thousand people actually purchased, whereas many companies made nothing, did nothing, and were truly worth nothing. On paper my stock options made me a millionaire, until the bubble burst, and since employees were in a six month SEC lockout and couldn't sell company stock, I watched my fortune actually drop below zero, as I had margined some money to pay for some music gear and was stuck with the bill and no stock to sell to pay for it.

I rented out my condo, gave away my furniture, put some things in storage, and took a bag and a guitar to New York City.

I couch surfed for the summer. There wasn't wireless internet yet so I'd wander around the corner to a coffee shop to check my email. I'd wash clothes at the laundromat across the street and watch beautiful East Village hipster girls I'd never talk to do their laundry.

It was a lonely city.

I found a place to live and moved into a Lower East Side five floor walkup on September 2, 2001. On September 11, 2001 one of the selling points of my apartment, the great view of the Twin Towers, was now two flaming buildings out of my bedroom window. My roommate and I didn't have a television so we listened to 1010 WINS, the twenty-four-hour news radio station, and tried to figure out what in the world was going on.

I was in the bathroom talking on the phone with a friend about the planes when they said that something was happening to one of the towers and I hopped with my pants around my ankles to the window just in time to see the first tower fall.

We walked to the top of our apartment building. We sat on the roof. People everywhere were on their roofs looking south at the smoke. An hour later the second building cracked and exploded like something you'd see in a Die Hard movie. People screamed. Ran. We were terrified.

I met a girl the night before who I would later move in with.

After the plane crash in Queens a month later, my dad called and told me to get the fuck out of New York City. But I didn't. I stayed. Went on tour. New York became a really expensive storage unit. My girlfriend and I grew apart. At least that's what I told myself.

In music, nothing else comes first. Nothing can, because you're always chasing the invisible carrot. There is always a chance that some choice, some thing, will change everything. You can't plan. You can't commit. You're never home. You're never anything.

I once flew to Cincinnati with my girlfriend and her family for a wedding. It was a Friday. My manager called to tell me she had a great gig for me in Massachusetts...on Saturday. I balked and she said if I was truly serious I would do what I had to do to make the gig (which was technically the right thing for a manger to say I guess) including getting on a plane and missing the wedding, which of course I did. And also, of course, the gig was shitty and no one cared and I probably sucked and I don't even remember who I was playing before but nothing changed and all I did was break my girlfriend's heart and probably some of my own too. And you can substitute any night in any town anywhere for that night, because that's what it's like most of the time. And sure, it's great when you have that transcendent moment and the six people in the coffee shop get it and it feels amazing and someone buys you a beer and maybe you fuck some girl but then your transmission goes out in Albany and it costs you two thousand dollars just to get back home and hating yourself doesn't really make you an artist.

I would never ever make those choices again. And I would tell any young artist that you do not have to slaughter everything decent around you to be great, or even to be mediocre, or even shitty. It doesn't have to be a bloodbath. To be great, one needn't be a fool.

But somehow ten years had gone by and many things happened and my father and Babette and I sit and watch a replay of an actual newscast from ten years before and I get to see what it was like for the people who had a television. We talk about how it was and I retell my story. And we get mad again and can't believe it again and are disgusted again and afraid again. But somehow it doesn't feel like anything has really changed in the last ten years. There was a brief time where I thought 9/11 might bring healing to the universe. Sadly, I think I was wrong.

John Attel tells me I should take the '41 into a brake shop to get the brake lines redone. The old lines aren't up to snuff and there are tubes that need to be run and we don't have the tools for that kinda stuff. John calls Leon and Leon calls a guy named Ernie and then Leon calls me.

"Ernie's Muffler and Brake. I called him and he said he could take your car right away, so get it over there."

I bring the trailer around from the backyard and strap the car down with tie downs. I hitch it on the van and drive with my dad to the brake shop.

Ernie and his son Junior are in the shop as I pull up next to the warehouse doors. I get my dad out of the van and put him in the shade of a big truck.

"Ernie?" I ask and shake his hand as he nods.

"Yes sir."

"Hi, Leon called you about my car."

"I just talked to him. What do you have there?" he asks looking out at the trailer.

"A '40." I say, which feels a little odd. We walk to the car. "So, I need brake lines and I need the drum brake hardware installed, but I have the hardware in here." I open the back door and shuffle through the Ziploc bags of springs and levers and such that I had bought at Auto Zone and separated into "left" and "right." I hand the bags to Ernie. "And I have the first part of the emergency brake cables that just go through the backing plate but I don't have the rest yet. And I need an exhaust."

"Well, we'll figure it out, and I'll just tie those up until you get the other cables," he's confident and I appreciate that.

"And the left back tire will probably go flat overnight. Just FYI."

"No problem. Why don't you pull forward and we'll roll it off the trailer."

I leave my dad in the shade and move the van. I unstrap the car and put the ramps down. A worker from inside comes out to push and I get inside and ride the car down the trailer ramps and into the parking lot until the car comes to a stop. We put two-by-fours back under the tires and leave it where it sits.

Ernie waves me inside, "Come on in and I'll get your information!"

"I'll be RIGHT BACK!" I call out to my dad, who's staring out into the parking lot, because that's the way I had left him.

Ernie has his phone out. "They brought me home from the hospital in this," he shows me a photo of a cherry red '40 Chevy coupe, "Just like yours."

My father turns sixty-nine. Truthfully none of us were sure he'd turn sixty-eight or sixty-seven or even sixty-six, but he has reached a lot of milestones in his life that we weren't sure he'd ever reach. He got married again. He walked my sister, albeit slowly with leg braces, down the aisle at her wedding. He got to meet his grandchildren.

Who knows what any of it's worth, truly. I hope there's an element of happiness for my father in those things, but it seems that really, those moments are for those of us left behind. Those moments exist merely so that we can remember them.

"Life AND death are for the living," one of my friends once told me. And I think he was right.

My dad doesn't want anyone to come over and celebrate, but Babette buys him his favorite cake anyway and my aunt and uncle and a few of his friends come by for dinner. We don't put any candles on the cake because my father can't blow out even a single candle, and he doesn't eat any cake of course because he can't eat even a single bite of cake. But we enjoy the day and are thankful for another year with my father.

The next day while cleaning up around the car, I roll the gas tank over and see and smell a spot of gas on the bottom of it. A tiny pinhole leak I think. It surprises me that the tank even has any gas at all if it was leaking and I wonder if I did it somehow after I took it out. I bring my dad outside so we can inspect it.

"New one," he says immediately.

"Are you sure?"

"New one." He is sure.

We order a tank online and it arrives within the week.

We wheel to the empty trailer outside to have a look at it. It's a light box. I pull a second box out of the shipping box and then pull out a shiny silver gas tank wrapped in plastic and hold it up in the air towards my father.

"Looks good, right?" I look at him for confirmation.

He nods.

I set the new tank down and grab the old tank from the ground and place it up on the trailer. I get up and straddle the old tank, pick up the new one, and hold it up over the old one to make sure the bolt holes matched up.

"Think we got the right one," I look at my father, "I think it's gonna look great."

I pull the sending unit and the filler tube out of the box and hold them up for my father to see. I read a bit of the instructions on how to measure and cut the sending unit to fit the tank. I turn the parts around in my hand examining them.

My father nods again.

Then we put everything up just like it came, and put the boxes in the garage. We'll tackle the tank when we get the '41 back with brakes.

We pack the van on a Saturday morning for another trip to Albuquerque for the annual Walk to Defeat ALS. Like just about every event, it seems, we can't believe that it has been an entire year since the last one. It's late September.

My father had a miserable night sleeping the night before. We put him in and out of his wheelchair twice. It's hard to get a reading sometimes on his cold fingers, but his oxygen was low and he could feel it. We tried to calm him down, probably grumpily, in the middle of the night. He finally fell asleep in his chair.

In the morning, his oxygen reads normal and we drive the four hours north through New Mexico. The drive is uneventful. We unload the van and check into the hotel. I'm excited that our team dinner is at the restaurant next door and I might be able to knock back a few glasses of wine and not have to drive the van back home. I'll just drunk drive my dad's wheelchair to the room.

But not an hour passes before my dad is asking to go to the hospital. I'm lying on the bed. A college football game is on the television. "Noooo, Dad, come on," I protest face first in the pillow. "We're gonna go and sit there for eight hours and they're just gonna send us home like every other time."

"Reee-lax honey," Babette always tells him, as if it's truly an option.

I go downstairs to the van to get the two small oxygen tanks we brought with us. There happens to be an ambulance and a fire engine on the curb. Someone's being wheeled out on a stretcher. I wonder to myself if it's another ALS walker. I flag down a couple firemen and ask them if it would be possible to come up to our room and just take my dad's oxygen and maybe reassure him and help him relax a little bit. They happily follow.

Firemen make me feel safe. Like they've got my back. Cops, from maybe a little too much television, often seem like they're a mustache away from tossing me in the county jail, whereas firemen make me feel like I've got a personal bodyguard. Besides and before the obvious selfless 9/11 stories, I had the privilege to attend an annual award ceremony where firemen, police officers, and private citizens were honored for their heroic efforts during the prior year. One of my friends was being recognized for calling the fire department and saving one of his friend's lives. Somehow he had woken up in the middle of the night and looked out his back window to see smoke coming from her garage apartment. It had turned out that she had come home late from a night of working music security at a venue and fell dead asleep wrapped in a blanket which caught fire after coming in contact with her radiator heater. At the ceremony, his friend recounted the story and thanked him and the firemen who broke her door down and rescued her from certain death. We listened to story after story of people being pulled from cars, burning homes, office buildings, etc. Stories of firefighters and police officers without question, and without fear, day after day, risking their own lives for others. It was an amazing night, and I was not surprised in the least when, several years later, hundreds of firefighters, and cops alike, lost their lives while valiantly attempting to save thousands of others from the burning World Trade Center towers.

The two young, strong firemen comfort my father as best they can. They take his oxygen level, which is a low eighty. If they do any more for us, they say, they will have to take my father to the hospital. My father decides against that, probably due to Babette and me whining about it. The firemen put a nasal cannula connected to the oxygen tank in my father's nose and leave without much fanfare.

We watch some more football. We put my father's breather on. We try to put both the breather and the oxygen cannula in his nose at the same time. Maybe an hour later we get a map at the front desk and drive to the nearest emergency room.

It's a calm Saturday night wherever we are in Albuquerque. The weather is about ten degrees cooler than El Paso and it feels perfect in September after the sun goes down. We wheel my father into the emergency check-in. We know the drill. They take his vitals. His oxygen has dropped into the dangerous seventies. They admit him into a room.

My father coughs a small but rough cough. His voice has all but disappeared into a faint and mostly unintelligible whisper. I say that out loud to him. The nurses take his temperature rectally because his mouth is so dry that he can't get his tongue off the bottom of it. They put him on oxygen and a hospital BIPAP. He is uncomfortable.

"HELP," he looks me in the eyes and says in small sharp muffled breaths, "HELP."

They x-ray for pneumonia. They start him on an antibiotic drip in the event that it's positive. The night emergency doctor comes in. He introduces himself and explains what they are doing.

"Does he have a DNR?" he asks me.

He does, of course, at home in the file drawer. "He does," I answer although not totally sure what else to say. "He does but lately we have been discussing the possibility of a trach tube but we haven't actually decided anything yet and..."

He looks at my father. "Do you have a DNR Mr. Sanders?" the doctor turns away from me and asks him directly and my father nods. Though I suppose we could just lie. I want to lie. This close to death, who wouldn't want to lie? Well, yes we have a DNR but my dad also said he would drive into the desert and blow his brains out if he ever had to sit in a wheelchair and you're looking at his wheelchair and is he really answering you with any clarity because the guy can barely breathe and now that we're at this point I'm certain he doesn't wanna die and I'm not sure he even answered the question for himself. It was almost like he was saying yes because I said yes and maybe he thought for a second that he didn't wanna die but somehow I was telling him that I couldn't do it anymore, or something like that, but they don't ask you like a therapist asks you. Hey gather 'round and let's talk about dying for a minute. They just wanna know if it's at home in the file drawer. And it was at home in the file drawer. But I wish it wasn't now. I wish there was no file drawer, and we didn't have to talk about it.

But that is all the doctor needs to know. He leaves and I turn to my father. I lean in over into his face, "DO YOU WANT A TUBE IN YOUR NECK? DAD I NEED YOU TO ANSWER ME. WE NEED TO KNOW IF YOU WANT A TUBE IN YOUR NECK." He looks everywhere except at me. "ARE YOU OK?" I ask him firmly. "YOUR LEFT EYE DOESN'T LOOK RIGHT." My dad twitches around but doesn't answer. His left eye seems to droop lower than his right, like maybe he had a stroke. "DAD ARE YOU OK?" I ask him again loudly and slowly. One eye goes one direction, the other goes another. Quickly but calmly the nurses get him a full face breathing mask and strap it around his head. His breathing evens out, his oxygen slowly goes up, the color returns to his face. Then he falls asleep.

He sleeps deeply. More deeply than he has in recent memory. It's a relief to see him rest. His eyes are half open. Babette sits beside him and rubs his head.

I call my sister in San Antonio. I email my brother who has saved up and taken a trip to Australia. I call my uncle who has left on vacation to Montreal. Everyone is far away.

The nurses come in with a catheter. I get up to wake my father. "Dad, I'm sorry to wake you up but they're gonna put a catheter in you ok? It's gonna be...not that great." I rub his gray beard. He doesn't respond. "Dad," I scratch his head. "Dad, we need you to wake up," I lean into him. I say again, "DAD I NEED YOU TO WAKE UP!" He breathes in and out. I lift his eye lids. "DAD! PLEASE WAKE UP! DAD PLEASE!" He is completely unresponsive. I turn to the nurse. I look at Babette. "Something's wrong."

"Something's wrong," I say again to the doctor who comes in the room, "He's not responding."

The doctor is calm. "Your father is in shock," he explains to me. "He's septic."

I don't know what that means.

"The x-rays told us he has pneumonia in his right lower lung and the infection has spread to his blood. His body is fighting right now. And that's why we've taken the action we've taken."

"It's like he's in a coma?"

"He's not in a coma," the doctor tells me, although I don't really know the difference.

"Ok, well what are our options?"

"There are no other options," he says flatly. "Your father has a DNR. It's not up to you or his wife. It's up to him and when I asked him if he had a DNR he nodded to me so we respect those wishes. He's in the last stages of a terrible disease. Right now we've got him stable. His oxygen is up. He's breathing well with the full BIPAP mask. We've given him the medicine he needs and now we wait twenty-four hours and see how his body reacts," he knocks on his head, "and we hope for a microscopic change."

A cold but accurate summary I suppose. It feels empty. I look at the floor and I start to cry. The doctor consoles me with a pat on the shoulder and leaves the room.

The nurse talks firmly and loudly to my father as if he is awake. "Ok, Mr. Sanders I'm here to give you a catheter! This might be a little uncomfortable."

"Will it hurt?" I ask her.

"There will be some pressure. It'll feel like he needs to urinate," and she lifts up his hospital gown and shoves what might as well have been a garden hose in his dick and feeds it through like it thought it was gonna come out his back.

I cringe and hold my father's hand. He doesn't so much as flinch.

The guilt hits me like a train.

I put my cheek to his cheek. I cry against his face. I smell his skin. I whisper in his ear. I apologize to my father. For ever yelling at him. For saying shitty things. For being lazy. For every time I grunted dramatically when I had to get up in the middle of the night to move him. For sighing when I had to get off the couch to give him a urinal. For throwing a fit. For questioning him buying a new water pump for the backyard, or a third winch. For refusing to change the colors on his legal database in 1996 to the ugly green and pink he wanted me to change it to, even though I'd still refuse those awful colors. For everything I actually apologize for and for everything I imagine I'm apologizing for. For everything that's real and everything that's not. And for everything else I'm forgetting.

And then I begin the rounds of phone calls. To my sister in San Antonio. To my brother in Australia. My uncle in Montreal. My cousin. My other cousin. I hold the phone up to my father's ear so he can hear everyone tell him to keep fighting and that they love him. Because the hearing goes last, they tell us.

I play him a message from Emory, "Hi gamma gamps. I love you gamps. I hope you get bettuh."

Babette and I sit on either side of the bed and talk over my father.

Our group of El Paso walkers all come to the room. We tell stories. We make jokes. We talk about whatever. We kill time.

We, including the doctor, don't think my father will make it through the night, but five hours later, sometime near midnight, he sleepily opens his eyes, and we all cheer.

My father is transferred to a non-emergency hospital by ambulance. I sneak over to the ALS walk Sunday morning, which happens to be close, to update our team and walk a couple laps around the minor league baseball stadium with about twelve hundred other walkers. We raise a hundred and ten thousand dollars for the Association, which beats last year's total by almost twenty-five thousand dollars.

We spend the week in Albuquerque. My sister flies in on Wednesday.

"Go home," I barely make out through my father's breathing mask.

"I know you wanna go home Dad, but you know we can't take you home like this. Your body needs to heal. The doctors won't let you out of here until you're ok to travel."

I wonder if he just doesn't want to die in Albuquerque.

He shakes his head.

"Are you ok?" I ask him.

He shakes his head again.

It's damn near impossible to understand him in the first place, but with a plastic mask muzzling his face, any chance of really communicating is lost. We start relying almost entirely on eyebrows, head nods, and a letter chart, which is the only real way for my father to say anything other than "Yes."

The chart takes patience. It's divided in half. Half of the alphabet on one side, and half on the other.

You ask my father, "Is it on this side?" and wait.

"Is it on this side?"

Eyebrows.

"Is it line one? Line two? Line three?"

Eyebrows.

"Ok, number three. Ok, is K? L? M?"

Eyebrows.

"Ok, the first letter is M."

And then you move on to the second letter. But he can't wear glasses with the mask on his face so he can't see the letters quite right, and sometimes it's like he's forgotten how to spell certain words, or he gets frustrated and just wants to stop and closes his eyes.

Babette works on a small computer as best she can. I sit on the hard hospital couch-slash-bed next to her and waste time on mine. I bring Starbucks for a cute nurse. There is nothing to do.

My father lies with his eyes closed for nearly the entire week.

I drive to the airport, which is just a couple exits down the highway, where you can watch the planes land and there is a good view of the sunset. There's a strong breeze. You can smell the rubber when the landing gear hits the runway. I walk away from the parking lot and sit in the dirt facing the sun with my camera. The sunset looks more beautiful to my eyes than it does to my lens.

Babette texts, "Are you coming back soon?"

"Do you need me?"

"The doctors want to talk to us."

I drive back to the hospital to an ICU doctor in our room. My father is asleep.

The doctor explains to us that while the pneumonia is improving, my father's respiratory system is not. He's dependent on the BIPAP, but we can't realistically keep a full face mask on him because the skin will break down underneath it the longer we keep it on his face. He isn't able to expel CO_2 fast enough on his own. His lungs are slowly failing. His recommendation is to trach my father immediately. He will give us time to talk about it and if we decide to do it he will take my dad to the ICU that night and sedate and intubate him until the morning when he will perform the surgery. The surgery, he tells us, is relatively simple and will only take about 15 minutes.

"But it's a different and more difficult level of care," he explains. "You should understand what it entails."

"We know," I assure him. And we do. We had already made the decision to care for my father twenty-four-seven. I already came home. I already sit beside him nearly all day every day. There are some variations in care with a trach, some subtle, some significant, but the hard part, the commitment, I thought, had passed. The doctor leaves us to talk.

My sister and I agree that we want a trach for my father, or that if it's up to us and he's unable to make the decision we will make it and that we are prepared to assume whatever responsibilities come with that decision. And we want him to consider that as he weighs his options. Our fear is that he is going to make a decision based on his current condition, which of course is still ultimately his prerogative, but the condition might improve if given the chance to heal and maybe that would mean he would make a different decision. But he can choose not to simply have a trach on a Tuesday and we will have to live with that.

I ask my sister and Babette for a few minutes with my father alone.

I scoot a chair to the side of his bed and lean into my dad who lies in bed with his eyes shut.

"Dad?" I hold my father's hand. "I just wanna make sure you can hear me."

Eyebrows. He is listening.

I can barely get the words out.

"Ok well, I, I need you to understand. I want to make perfectly clear to you that you are not a burden to this family. Ok? You are not a burden to me or Babette or to anyone else, despite what you think or anything that's been said, or anything that's happened. I am prepared and willing to care for you in whatever way you need to be cared for. Ok?"

His eyes stay closed.

I blubber through. "It is totally reasonable to consider other people when you make a choice like this, and I know you think that I gave up my music and photography and having a girlfriend or a family or whatever you think I did to come be here with you, but I need you to understand that there was never a tradeoff for me. It was never leaving one thing for another Dad. I need you to understand that YOU ARE NOT THE ONLY ONE WHO'S BENEFITTED FROM ME COMING HOME. OK? YOU ARE NOT THE ONLY ONE. OK?"

I continue. "Things evolve and this is simply the path that I've taken. Everybody takes a path, Dad. This is my path. I want to be clear, Dad. I love you, and I do not want you to die. I would prefer that you get a trach tube, but I will not interfere with *your* path if you decide your path is different. Ok? Ok Dad?"

I pause. "Dad?"

Eyebrows.

"Ok, so I have to ask you this directly Dad, because we have to tell the doctors what we want to do here. Ok?"

Eyebrows.

"DO YOU WANT A TRACH TUBE DAD?" I say loudly and directly to him.

And I wait.

I expect eyebrows, but instead my father shakes his head, "No."

I'm startled, actually, somehow expecting a quick yes. Imagining I'd call out for Babette and the doctors and they'd start prepping him for surgery.

"Did you say no, Dad?" I ask to make absolutely sure I understand him correctly.

Eyebrows.

I walk to the hospital lobby on our floor and call Eddie Okies. I stand in a corner away from another family. I tell him about my father's decision. Eddie suggests that while a trach tube in some ways would be a relief for my father—He'd no longer fight to breathe. Suctioning would be easier. There would be no mask on his face, and even in some ways it could be easier for the caretaker.—he isn't surprised.

With a trach now out of the question and my father not improving, there is only one real choice for us, we decide. Get my father home.

Eddie flies to Albuquerque from Portland the next afternoon. My aunt and uncle cut their Canada trip short. My brother is flying in on Friday from Australia and I let him know that he may need to change his flight and fly home to El Paso.

No doctor will release my father to drive home in our van, and even an ambulance home would be a tough ride through the middle of nowhere. It seems the only choice for us is to fly him home, but even a short medical flight home can easily run nearly ten thousand dollars.

A high school friend of my father's, George Butterworth, happens to call to see who my father will be rooting for in the UTEP-Houston football game. (My father went to undergraduate school at UTEP in El Paso and law school at the University of Houston.) Babette tells George about our hospital stay.

"Is there anything I can do?" he asks.

"Well, you wouldn't happen to know anyone in the medical transport business?" she takes a stab.

"As a matter of fact I do."

Fifteen minutes later we get a call from Elite Medical Transport in Las Cruces, NM. They offer to fly my father home to El Paso at cost. They'll be on standby and can be "wheels up" in an hour and a half.

Each morning in the hospital the nurses and doctors get together and discuss the patients on the floor. The plan of action. The day's work. The word on the floor is that we want to get my father home to El Paso. The discharge nurse comes by our room to discuss the details. The ICU doctor stops in, "I admire your choice, and I wish you a good day tomorrow on your journey home. Good luck."

I ask the hospital respiratory therapist to change the settings on our portable breathing machine to match the hospital settings so it will be the same when we get home. They call their legal department and the legal department refuses to let them adjust our machine. So I call the Phoenix based medical device representative who we had consulted earlier in the year to get information on the machine.

"Do you know anyone in the Albuquerque area that can help set our BIPAP?" I ask her.

"Actually," she says, "I'm getting off a plane in Albuquerque as we speak. I just moved here."

She's in our hospital room by the afternoon.

I have a wedding to shoot in Oklahoma City on the coming Saturday. I call a photographer friend in Dallas who without blinking agrees to drive the two-and-a-half hours from his house and shoot the wedding.

"I'm lifting you and your Dad up in prayer," he tells me.

"We need all the help we can get," I joke back to him.

After the wedding he will call to tell me that he won't take the money and is sending it all back to me to put towards the cost of my father's medical flight.

I tell my dad, "Tomorrow, we're flying you home."

Eyebrows.

"I'm gonna go back to the hotel and get some sleep, ok?"

Eyebrows.

The next morning the director of the New Mexico ALS Association delivers a check for half of the cost of the plane flight home. They had called a special meeting to disperse the money.

"That's why we're here, right?" she says.

"If you don't believe in the power of prayer," Babette tells me, "you need to have your head checked."

And while it's true, that in twenty-four short hours some very random and very necessary things happened that would enable us to get my father home to his city, to the house he built, to his family, and to his children, I can't help but think what I always think really, and that is if there is a god who is listening, who is acting positively on our behalf, who put a string of events together, who had a friend call about a football game that led us to an airplane, who had me book a wedding even though I would have a mad scramble to make it not fall apart but would ask someone who would actually do it and give me the money to boot, who moved a girl from Phoenix to Albuquerque to calibrate our breathing machine, who had the ALS Association call a special meeting to write us a check to help with the cost of our flight, then why couldn't the god have just stopped my father's terminal disease in the first place? Well, because there is no god. That's the only answer I can ever come up with that makes any sense to me.

But I tell her I will take it under consideration.

I get cream out to put on my father's cheeks to help the skin underneath his mask. I unhook the mask. It has pressed a deep purple rut in the right side of my father's face. I rub the cream into his cheek and skin comes off on my hand. It has begun to break down. I say something out loud but I wish I hadn't because I don't want my father to pay attention to it. I put his mask back on and pull it tight against the wound. My dad doesn't seem to feel it but I don't know how. I'm afraid that it won't be long before they have to administer medicine to fight that pain, and I don't want my father to merely get home, I want him to *know* he is home.

The medical team arrives that Friday morning around ten o'clock.

It takes a little more time than anticipated to get everything sorted out at the hospital and ready for transport but once my father is breathing well on a stretcher, we say goodbye to the staff and walk with him and the EMTs downstairs to an ambulance by the emergency entrance.

There is only one passenger allowed to fly in the plane and we decide that it should be Eddie Okies. He is a doctor, and that reassures us, but really I think he might enjoy a flight home with my dad just like they drove home together from college in Houston all the way across the state back to El Paso.

When the sun and the breeze hit my father's face he opens his eyes. We kiss him and tell him we love him and to enjoy the flight. My sister, Babette, my uncle Bill, and aunt Patsy all pile into the van with my father's empty wheelchair.

The flight is a quick hour in a Cessna 421. The drive is about four. Two hours into our drive I get a text from Eddie, "Flight was perfect. Your father is resting comfortably at home."

A hospice nurse meets us at our house. We fill out paperwork. We discuss the plan. We are given a phone number to call instead of 911 in case something goes wrong, and a bottle of morphine to give my father as it becomes harder for him to breathe. The nurse makes it clear that my father is dying.

The family comes. My brother arrives. Friends drop by. People bring food. Italian. Mexican. Syrian. My father sleeps in his bedroom and everyone takes turns going in to see him. He opens his eyes enough to see the visitors. He even laughs a muffled laugh inside his mask when my cousin and brother and I make dirty jokes, and then he coughs a nasty thick cough.

We give him Ativan to sleep. Eddie stays up all night standing next to him rubbing his head or sitting in a chair with his arm on my father's arm. My dad hums in his sleep.

"Aren't you tired?" I ask Eddie.

"I've done this my whole life," he says. And as a surgeon, I suppose he has.

The second day home my dad opens his eyes a little more. He seems more alert. But "It will get worse," Eddie tells me, "and as a caregiver you will want to make it better but there is nothing you will be able to do. It will be difficult. You will feel guilty. But just remember your job is to make him comfortable."

My sister flies back home to San Antonio because she has to work and needs to get back to her little girls. My brother works from our house for a couple days into the week and then also has to get back to work. Eddie flies back to Portland.

For my sister and brother it's a choice between leaving and risking not being with my father when he dies or staying and not knowing when he will die. But really it isn't a choice, I guess, because lots of times there just aren't truly any choices.

Later that night Mrs. Martinez calls to tell us that her husband, Mr. Martinez, has died. He choked while eating, she says. Everyone told him not to eat but he wouldn't listen and I couldn't really blame him for that. I remember how much he loved eating salsa at our support group meetings and how no matter how bad he choked he would just keep eating it. I hope it was salsa that did him in because I know he would have died happy.

My dad slowly opens his eyes more and seems to improve each day. He wants to move to the living room or outside to the porch, but Eddie says we have to be careful because he will only last about thirty seconds without oxygen before his oxygen saturation starts to go down and the portable oxygen tanks simply don't give him the oxygen that he needs for any real length of time. Any movement is taxing on him. Even turning him over in bed to change his sheets makes his blood pressure go up, and he has trouble breathing. We can't take him off the BIPAP either, so to move him out of the bedroom we put him on the portable breathing machine and also on a small portable oxygen tank that gives him just enough oxygen for the quick trip to the porch and then switch him back to the big concentrator once we get where we're going.

On the porch my uncle says, "This is like a slice of heaven." And it feels like it.

I become even more attached to my father's hip, though I didn't think it possible. I lie in the bed next to him with my laptop. Babette works in her office. We sleep and wake up and do it again. Eddie checks in twice a day on Skype, sometimes showing me diagrams of the nose and throat so I can more effectively suction my dad and see where I am actually sticking the tube. In some ways my dad seems like he was before the hospital. His eyes open wider and more often. He's more responsive. We are even able to sometimes switch him to a smaller breathing mask that covers just his nose, where he can finally open his mouth. I can clean his beard. It's easier to suction his throat.

The visitors taper off and I wonder when we will have to do it all over again.

The nights are a different story.

"H. Ok second letter. This side? This side? This side? One? Two? Three? Four? Ok M? N? O?"

Eyebrows.

"Ok O is the second letter right?"

Eyebrows.

"Ok third letter. This side? Ok five? Six? Ok six. U? V? W?"

Eyebrows.

"How. The first word is how?"

Eyebrows.

"Ok next word. Next word?"

Eyebrows.

"This side? This side? Ok five? Six?"

Eyebrows.

"U? V? W?"

Eyebrows.

"How W...How will?" I guess.

Eyebrows.

"How will we hear you if you need us?" I guess again, but based on the size of his petrified eyes I kinda feel it.

Eyebrows.

"Dad. I promise you. We will hear you. I'm ten feet away in my bedroom with the door open and Babette is sleeping right next to you. Ok? I promise."

Eyebrows.

"Are you afraid?"

Eyebrows.

"Of what?"

He mouths the words in his mask but I can't read his lips. Partially because they're obstructed, partially because he can't really form words anymore with his lips, and partially because there is so much air blowing in his mouth that it blows his lips apart.

"Of everything?"

Eyebrows.

"Are you afraid that you won't wake up?"

Eyebrows.

"Do you want something to help you sleep?"

Eyebrows.

Other than walking in the gate and not seeing the car, as it is still in the brake shop, I haven't thought too terribly much about the '41. I suppose at times I've imagined working alone without my father. Having no one to ask a question. Rolling out from under the car and looking up to nobody. And I had probably a while back realized that my dream of actually driving with my father in the car was maybe even always just a dream and that dream was fading, if not completely faded now that he was permanently attached to a breathing machine, an oxygen tank, and a catheter. In my head I had played out some of his strongest friends coming over and dramatically helping me carry him into the back seat and propping him up for a quick ride up and down the street, but that was really just a fantasy I suppose, as I can barely move him in his bed without it being hard for him to breathe. It had been three weeks, including our time in the hospital, since I took the '41 to Ernie's. I call him to get an update.

"The lines and exhaust are done," he tells me. "I'm just waiting on a cable to connect the brake pedal."

I wonder if maybe the car has just been sitting in the parking lot overstaying its welcome with a flat tire.

It's Friday. We've been home a week. I've switched my father to his old, smallest nasal mask. His oxygen is surprisingly good despite the lack of pressure the small mask gives him and the possibility that the air could just go in his nose and right back out his open mouth. You can see his entire face. I can put his glasses on him and we can check his email. Read some news. Look at some watches. He looks like my old dad. I can put a hot washcloth on his eyes. We even put him on a shower chair and give him a proper shower (mask on). I can scratch his neck and the back of his head.

My uncle and Vince and Butch come over for lunch and we stretch the oxygen tube all the way out by a tree, sit in the shade, and talk in the backyard for probably two hours. John Attel and his wife come over for dinner. My father asks me to play my guitar for him. We watch football. My father wears the small mask all day. He breathes well. It's his best day since we've been home.

At night we switch back to the full face breathing mask because my dad tends to sleep with his mouth open and the full face mask ensures that he will get the pressure and the oxygen he needs while he sleeps, but when I try to take off the small mask as we get ready for bed he shakes his head away from me.

"You wanna sleep with the small mask?" I ask him nervously.

He nods, gives me eyebrows, and mouths the word "Yes."

"Dad," I look him in the eyes. "You know I'm nervous about letting you sleep with the small mask. You know why we use the big one. You know it's possible that you'll sleep with your mouth open and your CO2 will go up, your oxygen will go down, and you may not wake up." I need to say it specifically and out loud.

Eyebrows.

I look at Babette. I look back at my father. Of course he knows. We've talked about it many times, but I can't blame him for wanting comfort. He'd had that plastic mask digging into his face for nearly two weeks.

"Ok. Well, then I want you to understand that if something seems wrong or your oxygen goes down or anything else I'm gonna switch you back to the big mask. Ok?"

Eyebrows.

I move his wheelchair to the side of the bed. I wrap the breathing tube, the oxygen tube, and his catheter tube around my body so that when I lay him down on the bed they'll fall into place.

"Ready?" I ask him.

Eyebrows.

And I put my hands underneath his arms and heave his bony body up out of his chair and turn him towards the bed and drop him into a seated position. His body slumps down as he waits for me to lay him back into my right arm and swing his legs up with my left until he lies flat on the bed. I put a pillow under his legs. I adjust and put pillows under his arms. I shift his head. Then I raise the bed up and roll one side of his pillow underneath his head to tilt it enough so he can see the television. I pull the sheet and the fleece blanket up to his shoulders.

"Feel ok?"

Eyebrows.

I tighten his mask.

"Too tight," he muffles back to me.

I breathe in and look at my father. "Dad, you know that we have to keep it a little tight so that the air doesn't leak out. You know that."

"Too tight," he says again.

So I loosen the straps a little bit around and on the top of his head and run my fingers underneath them to make sure they aren't pulling his hair or his beard.

"How's that?"

Eyebrows.

I kiss his forehead, "I love you Dad." I kiss him again and put my cheek to his mouth. His half puckered lips press against my beard and I smile, "I haven't felt that in a while."

I hadn't realized that because of the mask it has been at least two weeks since my father has kissed me goodnight.

"Gimme a couple more," I insist and he half-kisses my cheek as many times as he can.

I rub his forehead. He closes his eyes. I scratch under his neck with both hands. I kiss his head and his beard.

"I love you Dad," I say it again. "Ok I'm gonna get ready for bed."

Eyebrows.

And I give him one more kiss and leave the bedroom.

I fall asleep to the sounds of his breathing machine, the oxygen concentrator, and the air going in and out of the tubes.

We sleep all night.

On Saturday, October 8, 2011, my father dies.

Babette calls me frantically into the bedroom. We had both slept 'til 7:30. I scramble out of bed, but I know by the sound of her voice before I even get through the door what's wrong.

She's standing over my father in her nightgown. He's lying in his bed. His head is tilted to the left. His eyes almost closed. His mouth cracked open. Just as he slept. The breathing machine continues to blow air in his nose and out his mouth. His skin is pale.

I sort of shuffle to his bed in nervous half steps remembering what my grandmother's skin had felt like after she died. I kneel by the bed and slowly reach out and put my hand on his cold forehead.

I put my hands on my head. I stand up and walk in a circle, then down the hall and back into his room.

"I knew it," I say out loud to no one. "He wanted the small mask and I knew it."

"Do not do that," Babette says to me. "Do not. This is not your fault, and you know it's not your fault. Do not do that."

"I know I know I know I know."

I walk back to my father. I reach out and run my fingers across his forehead. On his beard. I feel the hair on his chest. I put both hands on his shoulders. I look at his eyes forcefully like maybe looking might make him open them. I lean in and kiss his cheek.

Babette nervously steps up to the bed and reaches behind my father's head and takes the mask off of her husband. She places it on the table next to the bed. Then she turns off the breathing machine. It goes silent, and not hearing it makes everything real.

I exhale and cry for my brave father.

Babette shakily picks up her phone and calls the hospice number and I go outside to call my family.

I call my uncle. I call my sister. I call my brother. I call Eddie Okies. Everyone calls everyone else. People are at the house almost immediately parking in the yard.

My uncle Bill wails for his brother at the end of his bed, "Oh Blu, you're really gone!" he cries.

A different hospice nurse arrives to certify my father's death. We stand around his body and watch her take his non-vitals and remove his catheter. My uncle says the catheter is the last thing keeping him from being free.

The hospice nurse calls our funeral home of choice and tells them to wait a couple of hours so we can have time with his body. More family comes. Friends too. People seem to want to spend a last few moments with my father before they take him away, and I don't think he would have minded.

The funeral home van arrives and after we say our last goodbyes, they wrap my father in his bed sheets and transfer him to a gurney. They drape a blue velour gurney cover with a gold "San Jose Funeral Homes" on it over him. I walk with them out the side door of the house and into the driveway to their gray minivan.

I point to one end of the gurney and ask the man in a suit, "Is this his head?" and he nods. I lean down and kiss the blue cover over my father and then they push the gurney into the van.

Watching my dad drive away in a funeral van is strange enough but what feels the strangest is that for the last eighteen months no one else has really driven my father anywhere but me.

My brother flies back in. My sister flies in with her family. She tells my little niece Emory that Grandpa is an angel in the sky, just like Lucky their dog.

And as far as I know, he is.

Eddie Okies said he read a book that talked about every event in the world being completely random and how we as humans only make up a narrative surrounding those events to cope with the randomness.

If that's the case, then this is my narrative.

I'm not sure my father knew he was going to die that night, but at the very least I think he knew that with the choices he was about to make, death was a real possibility. I've been told that the day before people die is oftentimes a great day. Now, I'm not sure if my dad intentionally had a great day or mentally had simply reached a place where it was easier to have a great day, but we had a great day, very relatively speaking, nonetheless.

For an entire morning, sunny afternoon, and night my father wore his smallest breathing mask. His face wasn't muzzled. He could open his mouth. Feel air on his face. He could put on his glasses. Read his email. Watch television. Almost be normal. When I look back at photos of him with his small mask, it looks like he's attached to a horrible machine with a tube sticking out of his face, but that day he looked like a human being to me. It was almost like he didn't have a mask on at all.

But my father knew very well the risk of wearing his small mask at night. He knew that there was a risk of him sleeping with his mouth open and the air going in his nose and straight out his mouth. He knew that without the mask as tight as it could be there was a risk of the air not getting into his nose at all. He knew that by not getting the right amount of oxygen and pressure into his lungs, he risked his CO_2 going up, and he knew that CO_2 could kill him.

And medically that's what I believe happened. I believe that the small mask was simply not enough to keep my father alive through the night. But there wasn't a struggle. There wasn't gasping for air, or at least he was unaware of his own suffocation. I believe my father was tired of being uncomfortable. He was worn out from the fight. To me, he presented his body with a test. Sustain me in the way that I choose, or do not sustain me at all.

But the most important part of my father's death is that my father was able to MAKE a choice.

One of the biggest challenges between ALS patient and caretaker is how to let the patient maintain some level of control over their life as they lose complete control of their life, and how to not take away that control by exerting your own control. At the end of his life, my father could not do a single solitary thing on his own, but, as far as I could tell, he did choose, ultimately, whether he lived or died, and for that I am thankful.

Everything in the house becomes a museum. The photographs, the wheelchairs, the garage, the bathrooms.

I go with my cousin to Home Depot and stand in front of the pipe fittings like a fool, looking for something to fix our air compressor. It hasn't been a day and I already need my father.

We make it to Monday and go to the funeral home to make arrangements. We will have a family visitation the next morning at the funeral home. My father will be cremated the day after in time for a memorial at our home. We give the funeral home a blue pinstriped suit, a pair of red and blue suspenders, and a red tie for my father.

I write my father's obituary and submit it to the paper. It's easier to write than I had anticipated.

Bluford (Blu) Sanders Jr. died peacefully in his home Saturday, October 8, 2011 surrounded by his family. Bluford was born in Paris, Texas on September 13, 1942 to parents Bluford B. Sanders and Margaret Lyon. He is survived by his wife, Babette Bailey Sanders, brother, William C. Sanders, twin son and daughter, Bluford (Blu) III and Erica Welch, son Luke, son-in-law Chris Welch and two granddaughters Emory and Hannah Welch.

Bluford was a lifelong El Paso resident, attending Coldwell Elementary School, Austin High School Class of 1960, and Texas Western University. He served with honor in the United States Navy. He earned a law degree from The University of Houston Law School and returned to El Paso to practice law for 40 years, the last 8 serving the citizens of El Paso as a public defender.

Bluford was an attorney by trade, but felt most at home with a tool belt around his waist, and a hammer in his hand. He was both a craftsman and a gentleman.

For seven years he bravely battled Lou Gehrig's Disease, also known as ALS, a disease with no known cause or cure, which is always fatal.

Our deepest thanks to Thelma Herrera and the El Paso MDA, Linda Ott and our ALS support group the Southwest Mountain Movers, Choice Hospice especially Linda, Evelyn, and Gabby, the El Paso Veterans Administration, and our fellow ALS fighters both living and deceased.

Join us Wednesday, October 12, 2011 at 4pm for a celebration of Bluford's life at his family home.

In lieu of flowers, memorial contributions may be sent, and are graciously appreciated, to our West Texas/Southern New Mexico ALS support group.

We meet my uncle the next morning at the funeral home. My father's rented casket lies at the back of an empty room with a piano and a television. Babette walks to my father first. Then my sister and brother. Then me. Then my uncle.

They trimmed his beard. Brushed his hair. His skin looks good. It's strange to see him lying like that. But not just that he's lying in a casket but that his head is straight, there's no mask on his face, and his hands are crossed at his waist, instead of turned up with his fingers curled.

My brother and I sit in a pew until our hour is up. I glance back at my father as I walk out of the room for what will be the last time, and we leave the funeral home.

We ask Kathy Cardone, the judge who presided over my father and Babette's marriage ceremony, to preside over his funeral. We spend the next twenty-four hours organizing food and photos and tables and chairs for the memorial. We figure my father's favorite place to be was in his own home. We had many great days in the backyard. There just doesn't seem to be a better place to honor him.

Cars line the street. More than two hundred people crowd into our backyard. My brother's childhood friend makes fajitas. We have our favorite Mexican restaurant bring appetizers. We buy lots of beer. Tragedy is fattening, I think to myself. My father's grade school friends come. His college buddies. His legal colleagues. Willie texts that his truck has overheated and he can't make the service. I tell him that he's welcome any time and that of course I understand. "He was like a father to me," he says and I know that he was.

Some of my friends fly in for the service and I remember how much it meant to my father when some of his friends came to his mother's funeral. It feels good to be around people that loved my Dad. Babette picks up my father's ashes from the funeral home and I carry them to the podium in the yard. That my father is now only ashes in a box is surreal, and I'm surprised at their weight.

My uncle gives a speech. Kathy speaks. Lawyers. Friends. Eddie Okies.

I speak:

Hi everyone. I want to welcome you to my father's home and the house that I grew up in. I'm Blu the third or Little Blu. On behalf of my stepmother Babette, my twin sister Erica, and my brother Luke, I want to thank you all for being here. We've had many wonderful evenings on the porch and in the backyard together as a family and with friends. When we were mulling over where to have this memorial we decided there was no better place to get together.

Many of you knew my father as a lawman, but I knew him as more of a craftsman. He loved his tools. He loved his garage. He built much of the house behind you with his own hands. He built that building over there. He built the building behind it. He framed and roofed that tree house behind you just like you would frame and roof a real home. Many people always ask how my father knew so much about so many things and the answer is, nobody really has any idea. But he could do your divorce or he could dig up your yard and put your sprinkler system in. He was a damn good artist, photographer, and in his legal line of work, an orator. He was the definition of a renaissance man.

But I made it very clear to my father over the last few weeks before he died, that although I've learned many many things from him, from how to weld (poorly), to how the air conditioning works, to how to sue your landlord (very helpful!), there was absolutely nothing more valuable to me than to watch and learn from his example of sheer bravery and unfathomable patience as a terminal disease took his ability to swing a hammer, to walk in this yard, and even to kiss my cheek.

As his disease progressed and we couldn't leave the house as often, one of his favorite things to do was sit on the porch. We'd wheel out here and just sit. Watch the hummingbirds. Listen to the wind chimes.

I want to share a story with you. There was one day in particular when we were sitting on the porch looking out into the backyard. It was a day not unlike today. A beautiful El Paso day.

There was a breeze. The sun was going down. I never knew the best time to talk about life and about death with my father, but it seemed like the right moment, so I looked at him and asked, "What are you thinking about Dad?"

And he paused. He looked into the sky and back out into the yard. And I'll never forget what he said.

He said, "I think we need to build a retaining wall there against the back fence, about two feet high, all the way from corner to corner."

Thank you so much for coming and please enjoy yourselves, share your stories and have a good time, because I can assure you that my father wouldn't have it any other way in his home.

We have a slide show playing on the TV in the living room. It's both fun and painful to watch the photos go by. My father was a good looking rugged young man with a big smile and an infectious laugh and you can see it in the photos, but you can also see the deterioration of his body as the years flipped by and ALS tore that body apart.

As funerals go, I think we threw him a pretty good one. It was already going to be sad, I told people, why make it any sadder?

But the house is soon empty. A few days after the service everyone has left town and people don't come by as often. There are loads of leftovers still in the fridge.

It's completely silent as we sleep.

I hitch up the trailer and drive to Ernie's after I drop my sister at the airport. The '41 has been sitting in his parking lot for a month now. Two weeks because that's how long it took, and another two because my father was getting sicker.

I tell him about my father. We walk out to the parking lot. I poke around the car and can see the new brake lines winding around to the front drums. I reach inside the car and push the brake pedal with my hand. The silver exhaust sticks out from under the back of the car.

We push the '41 up and on to the trailer and strap it down. I pay a reasonable five hundred and fifty dollars for the work. I think it's too cheap and I tell him so.

"That's what it costs," he assures me, but I don't believe him.

"Slowly but surely!" I smile and say as I shake his hand and thank him.

"That's the way it goooes."

The next week I take a twelve hour train ride to San Antonio to see my mother who's visiting my sister on her fall break from teaching school. I've seen my mother maybe twice in the last two years. The train winds into southwest Texas. Terrain that, despite growing up basically around the corner, I have never really seen. I've never camped in Big Bend. Never seen the Marfa Lights. Never really went too much in the opposite direction either. Maybe that's just what happens. You sorta take everything around you for granted, and somehow you go your whole life without really looking around your own neighborhood. It's a long haul, but I get to breathe a bit, watching my state chug by county by county.

"Do you feel any relief that you don't have to turn around and rush back?" my mother asks me on the way home from the train station.

"Not really," I say. And I don't. Though time I all but begged for while my father was alive, I had instantaneously gotten more time than I ever really wanted. I feel myself already just wanting to go home.

"I'm sorry honey," she says to me. And I know she is. My mother is a sweet, kind, compassionate, woman. And while she had a messy divorce from an incompatible relationship with my father, she hated to see him suffer, and I know that it has to be strange for her too.

Carlos calls.

"Mi papá murió," I tell him because I had looked up the past tense of "to die" months before, knowing that I would have to tell

242

him at some point. I want to say so much more, but my Spanish is too rudimentary and I feel stupid because of it.

"I sorry," he says back to me in his even worse English. I wish that we could both talk to each other like regular people in any language.

"Estoy en San Antonio. Llamame en la próxima semana." *I'm in San Antonio. Call me next week,* I tell him.

The week goes by in a haze. I play with my nieces, run errands with my mom, spend a couple days with my brother in Austin, and fly home to start sorting things out at the house.

With the '41 back in the carport, I put my work boots on. I put my work shirt on. I open the garage and I stand in front of the cardboard box with the new silver gas tank in it. I slide the tank out of the box, and then out of its plastic. I set it on the end of the trailer behind the '41 which I had left strapped down not knowing if I would need to haul it somewhere else any time soon.

I walk to the toolbox and stand by myself. I open the drawers and pick out a few sockets. A socket driver. A few screwdrivers. My dad isn't there to nod or to shake his head that, "No, that's not the right tool, Son," and I miss that.

I pull the sending unit out of the box and stare at it for a few minutes. You're supposed to trim it based on the depth of your tank. I measure the tank. I read the chart on the instructions but I'm still not sure how to cut the thing. I call the company and they walk me through it. Bolting it on seems simple, but the holes don't seem to line up correctly and it takes some time. I get it as tight and as in the right place as I can and hope that gas or vapor or whatever won't leak out. The filler tube fits about the same.

The tank itself takes just the three bolts to install. I put my tools near me and I lie on my back on the trailer, put the bolts on my stomach, lift the tank onto my chest, and shimmy under the car.

I lift the tank up and into the cavity where it mounts. I wedge the filler tube up and into its hole in the frame and it holds the tank in place when I let go. I slide the tank above the new exhaust. The exhaust curves under the gas tank perfectly as if Ernie knew exactly where the tank was going to be after it was installed. It takes me almost two hours to put three bolts into the tank, but shines a brand new silver when I push myself out from under the car, off the trailer, and squat down to look up at it.

My first instinct is to run inside and get my father and wheel him out to show him my work.

I can hear the music of the ice cream truck in the distance pulling down the street. It stops in front of my house and I walk out the gate towards it. It's nothing fancy. Pretty beat up. But the music plays, and the ice cream is cold, and that's all that matters. This is not just any ol' ice cream truck. This is Joe's ice cream truck and Joe is the short, sun-browned, friendly as can be, Mexican ice cream man I've known since I was in junior high school when he would park across the street from school and we'd all run over to him and eat Lemonheads, Sno-Cones, or something else terrible and amazing for lunch.

The music stops and Joe climbs down from his truck to meet me in the front yard and hands me a sympathy card and a hug from his family to mine.

Some twenty-five years ago, Joe tells me, he was selling ice cream at the soccer fields in Canutillo down the highway from El Paso. The park wanted to kick him out since he wasn't approved to sell anything. My father, who was there coaching my young soccer team, helped him strike a deal to give a percentage of his sales to the park so he could stay and sell ice cream to the kids. When he came to my father with the share of the first day's sales, my father told him to keep the money and paid for it himself.

Joe would call my father from time to time for legal help when someone in a position of authority, like an overzealous junior high school principal, would get power hungry and demand he move his truck from one side of the street to the other, and when that wasn't enough to go away completely and back and forth and back again.

Joe still stopped by the house on occasion twenty-five years later to bring my father a box of his favorite Mexican coconut popsicles that we all hated, as none of us kids liked coconut, much to my father's utter bewilderment each time we told him. There are still coconut popsicles in our refrigerator.

Carlos comes through the gate the next morning while I'm cleaning up outside. I walk to meet him. I figure he's looking for work, but instead he offers a, "Lo siento, Blu," and gives me a big bear of a hug.

"Gracias, Carlos," I say to him. He's here to offer his condolences for my father.

"Adelante," I say with a shrug. *Forward.*

"Así es la vida," he agrees. *That's life.*

I pull my phone out and open the translate app, "Un momento," I ask him to wait while I type. Then I hold my phone out to him to read and I say, "Trabajó a través de ti." *My father worked through you*, I tell him.

"Gracias," he answers and nods his head. I know he hurts too. "Puedo saludar a Babette?" he asks me. He wants to say a little something to my stepmother.

"Claro que sí," I say of course and motion him inside the house.

He gives Babette a big hug and says he's sorry. Babette cries. She knows that Carlos and Willie weren't just workers at my father's home. They were his hands. I think Carlos knows that.

I ask him to come back Saturday and put the door jam and the door back on my father's bedroom because we don't need to fit a wheelchair through it anymore.

I drive to the San Jose Funeral home and pick up my father's death certificates stacked in a fancy burgundy folder with gold writing on the front. I stand on the sidewalk and cry as I read the forms. It's official, I think to myself.

Dying comes with paperwork. Even when there's nothing too terribly complicated there is still a lot to do. Cancel phone service, bank accounts, car insurance. No one takes your word for it. Everyone wants proof.

My father had a few thousand dollars in the bank, which would be gone not too long after paying bills and such. He had no life insurance. No retirement payout. He had only his home, that was paid for, and which he had asked me once, while sitting on the back porch and looking out into the yard, to "please never sell," his tools, a few pieces of jewelry, and a small gun collection.

None of his children, including me, have ever wanted to make a life in El Paso, and I'm not sure Babette sees herself there long term either, but we hadn't yet sat down and talked about the details or much of anything really. Babette is busy. The business she owns with her brother just declared bankruptcy. They were being sued. It's been a shitty month.

October disappears. November comes and goes. Thanksgiving is much harder than I had anticipated. Christmas is right around the corner, and I don't expect it to be any easier. The holidays are difficult, people told me, and they were exactly right.

It gets cold again. I take a weekend camping trip with my cousin and his wife and baby boy to the hot springs in the Gila National Forest, not too terribly far, as the crow flies, from El Paso. We sit in the springs. We jump naked into the icy Gila River like fools. We sit in our jackets by the fire. I think of how my father would have slept well in the cold.

I write a poem in my head.

In the Flame

I sat in the cold next to the fire

I looked for my father in the flame

In the smoke

In the sky

In the stars

But I saw nothing

I listened for my father in the trees

In the river

In the silence

But I heard nothing

But when I tried to feel my father

In my head

And in my heart

I felt something

The holidays pass. They, like everything else, seem empty without my father. Yet in some ways he just doesn't seem gone. I say out loud many times how I can't believe that my father is dead even as things move forward. But that's what things do, I think, whether you want them to or not. I remember looking down my street the day after my father died and watching the traffic in the distance. It didn't stop. The cars passed and they travelled to wherever it was that they were going and presumably arrived at their destinations. The next day the garbage would be picked up. People would still go to work. The world would simply continue to spin both metaphorically and quite literally not acknowledging in any real way that my father was no longer alive. It was a strange realization that, really, no one but us paused in tribute.

Two thousand and twelve arrives. As with most years, I can't believe it's two thousand and whatever year it happens to be. And then, suddenly, I get a job that takes me out of El Paso.

I call a friend, who tour manages a band, looking for work.

"It's about that time," I say to him.

He points me to another tour manager, who I had met a time or two, who ran the Miranda Lambert tour. Miranda was a successful, firecracker of a female country artist who I'd known a bit as her producer was my music publisher in Nashville. She was known in the industry for doing things her way, which as far as I could tell, she actually did. She was one of the handful of country artists that rang authentic. Her band was from Texas, as were some of her long time crew. I explain to her tour manager that my experience on the road was a little heavy on the beer drinking, womanizing, lazy mediocre guitar playing side, and rather light on the actual tour work experience side, but he tells me it isn't rocket science and that I'll get the hang of it and I can have the job if I want it. That was a Wednesday. I leave two days later.

The tour will be steady through the spring and then if it's working out, I can stay on into the summer and fall. It will criss-cross the country, and even possibly leave the country, although most people don't realize that while touring takes you to so many places, you hardly see a thing.

I pack my father's Suburban with some of his tools for my brother, a few of my sister's childhood toys for my nieces, and drive it to San Antonio. She needs a bigger car for her family and I can't even afford to put gas in that guzzler. I'll fly to Nashville from there. It feels strange getting things of my father's together to give away. It doesn't seem right. They don't seem like ours, even though technically they are now. I wonder if he can see me from somewhere divvying up his possessions, and if it makes him angry, or satisfied, or sad.

The morning I'm supposed to leave I stand in Babette's office and cry.

"I'm not ready to leave," I tell her.

I don't feel ready to leave El Paso. I don't particularly want to be on the road again, and I definitely don't want to leave the '41. In my head I flash forward and see it sitting in the same place on the trailer a year later, or a year after that, or even longer.

"You have to do this," she says to me and gets up from her desk to give me a hug.

"I know," I say. And I guess I do.

After the first weekend it's clear that this will be the most exhausting job I've ever had. I'm the Production Assistant, or PA, which is non-stop and non-glamorous; servicing the needs of all seventy people on the tour. Days are long starting at 7:30am and winding down somewhere around one in the morning. I snap photos if I have a few minutes during a show. My feet hurt. There isn't much sleep.

My father would have loved our tour buses. He would send us kids emails during the holidays with links to the two million dollar Prevost he wanted for Christmas. He once parked next to a Deftones bus in an El Paso arena parking lot and was having a look. The band opened the door and brought him on and showed him around. A gesture I always appreciated, and I wish that I could send him a photo of all eight of ours.

After two weeks I come home for a short break.

I stop by John's dealership to see what he thinks about the car.

"I'll come by this weekend," he says, "and we'll see if we can get her started. Fill up a gas can."

I had ordered a new shifter for the transmission while I was on the road and the brown box is on my desk when I get home. The shifter is fairly simple to install. It's a metal frame that straddles the transmission, along with the shifter knob that comes up through the floorboard into the car. I had removed the middle piece of the floorboard months back as the new, bigger transmission was rubbing up against it. The shifter is connected by a rod to the shifter pawl. When you move the shifter from park to drive, for example, the rod pulls or pushes the pawl, which is connected to the gears inside the transmission. I put the shifter together according to the instructions, mount it on the transmission, and send a photo to John for confirmation.

"Nice!" he replies.

John is over on the following Sunday afternoon with a car battery, a battery charger, some battery cables, and a cone shaped measuring cup in hand. Doug joins when he sees something is up from his front yard.

"Get me a screwdriver and some pliers and the gas can," John instructs me.

He sets the heavy battery on the trailer next to the car. Takes the positive battery cable and connects it to the solenoid. The solenoid is what gives the starter power to start. He grounds the negative cable to a bolt on the engine. He connects the battery charger to the battery. Then he runs a piece of gas line into the gas can. He fills the measuring cup with gasoline and hands it to Doug. Doug already knows what he's supposed to do with the gas. He takes off the air filter over the carburetor.

Then John takes some gas line and fashions a loop out and back into the transmission. Normally there would be a transmission cooler where the transmission fluid would exit, be cooled, and then go back into the transmission. But, "we'll be fine for now," he says to me.

John stands on one side of the car. Doug stands on the other with the cup of gasoline ready to feed the carburetor.

I back up and stand in front of the car making a video with my phone.

Then John places the screwdriver on the solenoid to complete the circuit from the battery and act as an ignition switch—commonly known as he hot-wired it.

There's a spark. A snap of electricity. Some clicking. The engine turns over but doesn't start. Doug waits to pour. John closes the circuit again. The engine turns and turns. It's trying. He's reaching over the engine and pumping the lever where the accelerator will eventually connect while he's giving the engine electricity from the battery. He tries once more, and then, just like engines do, the 250 rumbles to life.

John pumps the lever, Doug feeds gasoline into the carburetor, and the engine purrs.

"Well," John looks back over his shoulder to me with a smile and says casually, "It runs."

It's a sweet sound to be sure. I suppose I wasn't really sure if the engine would start in the first place. It had been sitting out in the elements in the carport for well over a year, and who knows for how long before that. But it did. And that's big. The biggest, maybe.

John lets it run for a minute, then he pulls the gas line out of the can and lets the engine stop.

"Sounds pretty good," Doug says and John agrees.

We decide to reconvene in February. I'm leaving for another two weeks.

The tour takes us to Charlotte, Baltimore, Charlottesville, and East Rutherford, New Jersey. I stay on in New York for a few days, since I'm taking the next weekend off to shoot a wedding in Austin. It has been a few years since I've been to the city, the last time with my father and Babette.

I stay at a friend's apartment which has no kitchen or shower, although that sounds perfectly reasonable to me for New York City.

I get a hotel on the last night for some privacy. I walk around Times Square alone. I eat a slice of pizza. Drink crappy deli coffee and love it. I wander over to the Westside Highway and take photos of the sunset as it dips behind the Intrepid aircraft carrier. I sit in my hotel room in my underwear. I write while trucks pass and sirens wail. I fall asleep to the honking horns.

My February disappears without any car work and I leave for another two weeks. I pick up a radiator, which I had bought from Emmit Radiator, a local radiator shop, who had it made to spec from somewhere in California, on my way home from the airport on my next break. I push it under the car for safekeeping.

George Butterworth, my father's high school friend who helped us with our medical flight from Albuquerque, goes to the doctor to find out he has metastasized cancer throughout his body and dies three weeks later.

I leave again for the entire month of March. April arrives. I still haven't done any more work on the car and I'm leaving for most of the rest of that month. I decide to call Ernie.

The '41 hasn't left the trailer, which isn't great for progress, but makes moving it easier. I borrow my cousin's truck as I don't have anything to pull my trailer now that my sister has my dad's Suburban. I make a slow drive to Ernie's and arrive safely.

I give Ernie a rundown of what I have left to do – install a gas pedal, repair the floorboard, and a handful of miscellaneous details yet to be finished.

"You're not in a hurry?" he asks.

"Nope. I'll be gone for another month."

"Well, let's pull it down."

Babette calls in tears from the veterinarian's office as Little Fella had a stroke and was unable to move his back legs, could not eat, and could not so much as lift himself up to go to the bathroom. He will be put down and his giant tail will not thump the wall like a bat when I walk in the front door. Make way doggie heaven. A hundred and sixty pounds of German Shepherd comin' atchya.

Our spring tour ends with a themed end-of-tour party. Our bus's theme is "Pure Country" the movie, and as the newest member of the crew I'm generously given the role of Leslie Ann Warren's Lulu Harris, complete with a tacky early nineties ensemble, red lipstick, and a wavy brown wig. And although this leg of the tour is technically over, after another week home I'll leave yet again for a month and a half, and we will continue dates into September. The '41 is unknowingly being pushed into the summer, and I wonder if the summer will turn into the fall.

And the summer blisters by indeed. It's the hottest year on record. My trips home become a blur.

The tour leads us all the way to Anchorage, Alaska where the National Guard takes us on Blackhawk helicopters through the stunning Alaskan landscape and over breathtaking glaciers on a day off. I wish that I could call my father to tell him all about it.

There still sits on the wall facing the stairs to the second floor of our house a photo of him and his longtime friend and naval pilot buddy, Larry Duthie, who was shot down and rescued in Vietnam, and who once took my father for a ride in an A-4 Skyhawk fighter plane.

"If given the chance to have sex with a different woman every day for the rest of your life," my father once told me, "or to take a ride in an A-4, take the ride in the A-4."

He would have loved to hear about my flight in the helicopter, and how I sat in the gunner seat with the window open and my camera hanging around my neck.

We play in eastern Washington and on my way home for a break I stop through Portland to spend a few days with Eddie Okies. We have strong coffee, good wine, and mention often that my father would have loved this or that.

September comes. I have ten days off. I pay Ernie with cash and some cold Bud Light and tow the '41 back to my house to begin what I think will be the simple reassembly of the splash guards, fenders, and hood, but of course turns into me calling John Attel multiple times a day when the fenders don't quite line up, certain bolts don't fit where they're supposed to fit, and the radiator bumps up against the engine fan. I end up taking everything apart again and laying it back on the ground while we send the radiator and the bracket that holds the radiator in the car to a machine shop to get it adjusted to give me some more room between it and the engine. Emmit Radiator reattaches the bracket and repaints the radiator for me before I take it home and slowly piece the fenders back together. I had snapped some photos the year before while taking everything apart in hopes that it would help me put everything back in the right place, but I didn't take nearly enough photos, and everything seems like it could go on in five different ways. After putting on and taking off the fenders, and splashguards, a few more times, the body starts to stabilize from wobbly metal to a solid front end. I find the radiator rods that additionally support the radiator from just under the dash in the trunk and after twisting some bolts together, grab the bars with my hands and pull. Nothing moves.

"I'm impressed," John tells me when he comes over to inspect my work.

Giovanni's sister helps him, in slow motion, turn his legs up and out of his car and his body into her arms as she balances him and he straightens up and holds onto the door, while his brother brings his manual wheelchair around from the back of the car for him to sit.

Linda and Gene Ott introduce me to his family. His father-in-law and sister have made the trip from Juarez with Giovanni. Only ninety minutes waiting to get across the bridge, they say. His younger brother has flown in from Houston, and his older brother lives not far from us just over the New Mexico border in Santa Teresa.

The sister wheels Giovanni to the group. I reach my hand to his. He has hardly any strength left in his grip. The skin has already smoothed from lack of use.

"I'm Blu," I say, looking him in the eyes, "It's my pleasure to meet you."

"Iiiit iiiis niiiice to meeet yooou," Giovanni says in perfect English, albeit, a slow ALS English. Good English is not surprising from a thirty-four-year-old urologist from Juarez. He has two young children and a doctor wife back in Mexico. He had been diagnosed fourteen months prior and the progression was rapid. His legs are weak. He cannot stand. His head is mostly straight but you can see his neck starting to tilt. He looks so young. Younger than his age. He smiles sweetly. Sweeter than maybe I might have smiled on a trip to another country to meet a set of strangers who would give me equipment to help me as I died. Equipment that a stranger gave my father to help him as he died and would be passed on to others after he too died.

It occurs to me that ALS doesn't recognize borders.

Giovanni had surgery for Carpel Tunnel Syndrome thinking that his wrist issues were, like most people would think, surely not a sign of something deadly. I wonder if as a doctor he sees his disease differently, as his body shuts down and he watches the changes. Based on his own research, he has opted against a feeding and a trach tube. He will eventually starve to death or stop breathing. He knows this before he meets anyone from our support group.

Gene Ott has told the family, "It's ok if you change your mind. Just remember that."

We walk inside the house and then the gentlemen walk to our back storage building where we have stored all of our handicap equipment. We carry several plastic boxes back to the house, a shower chair, the BIPAP machine, and then push a wheelchair through muddy grass because the battery has died and it has just rained.

I'm a little rusty, but go over the equipment with the group, explaining what each thing does, and suggesting that they don't have to take anything and that hopefully something things won't be necessary. I am blunt when I talk about things like the plastic toilet, or jamming a wand into a throat to suck the phlegm out. But there is no use sugar coating anything. They need to know and I need to tell them.

One wheelchair is brand new. My father had been fitted for one earlier in the year before he died, and it took so long to get it that when we finally did he was bed-ridden and we had no real time to use it. It sat in our big bathroom for nearly a year.

Lifting a powered wheelchair is nearly impossible, even with several men. Gene Ott will bring ramps by the next week and we'll get the chair in a truck and to Giovanni in Mexico. I wish that I could go, but it is still dangerous to go to Juarez. I hope that no one will stop the truck at gun point and demand the chair.

"You. Are. A good man," Giovanni's sister says to me in choppy English, as she pushes her brother back down the driveway to the car.

His sister will help care for him. His father-in-law will spend two weeks a month at the house and his father will drive in from Chihuahua for the remaining two.

"Thank you," I offer, pat Giovanni's back, and say to her, "but he's the good man."

"Miii caaasa es sssu caaasa," Giovanni slurs to me with a soft smile, looking up slowly from his wheelchair. *My house is yours.* A long common Spanish phrase of friendship.

"También," I say right back to him. *Mine as well.*

With time a little more on my side, I schedule a proper VIN inspection for my time home, borrow John's Suburban, and tow the '41 around the mountain (I'd always been too scared to tow it over), not too far from Leon's junkyard, in the quiet dim morning light to a city office nowhere near any other city office, at six thirty in the morning on a Wednesday, because Wednesdays are when they do inspections, and I am told the inspectors are friendlier in the mornings.

I never really get to see the sunrise since I live on the west side of the Franklins, and a cool quiet desert sunrise is a fair consolation for getting up early. There are two people already in the parking lot, although my appointment is first. I pay the forty dollar inspection fee, sit on a plastic chair in the waiting room, and wait. Retired Officer Seelig comes through a half door and walks me out into the parking lot where I point to my car. He shows me around as he inspects and explains what he looks for. Talks to me about VINs. Tells me that they'll really be looking at the engine since that's newer and there's no record of the '41 in the VIN database. He had checked the day before.

The inspection is quick. I wait again in the lobby while Officer Seelig searches for information on my engine. In only a quick few minutes I'm handed a clean VIN inspection report for a reassembled 1940 Chevy, ready to be submitted to the DMV for a title application. I shake hands and thank the officer and walk back out to the parking lot.

I sit alone in my car as the sun comes up and get tears on the form in my hands.

"Peanuts can do it."

That's pretty much what I always heard when I asked John, Leon, or Eddie Solis about the next step in making my car run. Electrifying it. Making the gauges work. Turning on the lights. Starting the car. That kinda thing. Peanuts is a retired Vietnam Vet who dabbles in car restoration and is an expert in wiring. He does it one car at a time, when he feels like it, in his garage, which happens to be a stone's throw from Leon's junkyard.

Leon puts me in touch. Peanuts and I have a couple chats on the phone. I get a list of parts he will need and I have them shipped to his house. John tows the '41, while I'm on the road, across the mountain to Leon's junkyard. Peanuts will come get the car when the parts come in.

"I think I also need to bring you a battery," I suggest to him.

"Ah, there's no battery?"

"Well, no. Or an ignition switch."

"You can get those anywhere," he says. "And get a top post battery."

On my next trip home I take the battery and the ignition switch and drive them to the northeast side of town.

It's evening and there are six or eight guys drinking beer on the sidewalk when I pull up to the house. Peanuts lives in a small unassuming brick home in a simple residential neighborhood. Many of the yards are landscaped with painted rocks and concrete, a common choice in the desert where lush green yards can be quite pricey. You can see Leon's place if you look out from the driveway across an open lot. There is a sanded-down empty car body sitting on a frame, which looks Chevy-ish to me in the driveway. Peanuts opens the garage door and walks out to open the chain link fence to greet me. He has dark skin, maybe Puerto Rican, short gray hair, and a mellow vibe. Talks calmly. Laid back.

He takes me into the garage where he has a beautiful blue '57 Chevy kept out of the elements.

We walk to the big box of parts which I had shipped to him. He opens it to show me the contents.

"Everything looks good for the most part. Here's your harness," he holds up a snake of red, yellow, and black wires. He hands me a small box. "That's your turn signal," I pull it out and look at it. "Reducer," another box.

We talk about the rest of the stuff. He shows me where the ignition switch will go. Where he put a horn in his Chevy. Says we can get one from Leon.

We talk a bit more about his cars. He has a thing for vintage scooters. How he has beaten prostate cancer. "Agent Orange," he says. And many many other Vets probably also say.

He tells me Leon will tow the car over in the morning and he'll get to work, and that he had actually been over to have a look at the car already and was surprised at how good of shape it's in.

"Well, it was in a garage for years," I tell him. "Dusty, but overall in pretty good condition." I tell him the story of the car. About coming home for my father. About how he was sick.

"Is he still alive?" he asks.

"No, unfortunately. He's not," I explain. "He had ALS. Six years though. That's long for ALS."

Peanuts pauses for a moment. "How strange," he says. "We just buried my younger brother. He lived seven years with ALS."

But ALS is a rare disease we are told.

I leave again for the last two weeks of the tour. There's no wild party. No big goodbyes. Everyone is exhausted and wants to get home. I leave the sunrise in Birmingham and fly home to El Paso. I watch the clouds change from colors to white and the terrain from green to brown, like it always does on my way west.

I call Peanuts from the parking lot.

He surprises me with, "Bring some gas and transmission fluid and we'll see if we can get her started."

I drive home, dump my bags, grab a gas can, stop for some transmission fluid, top off the can, and head over the mountain.

The '41 is in his driveway, looking not much different than it did in my own driveway. Peanuts walks to the gate again to meet me and we both walk over to the car.

He points into the engine compartment and the new multi-colored wires. "There's your wiring harness," he says, pointing to the black plastic box with two rows of labels, "Lights" and "Gauges." And then to the other side of the car. "And your battery box. I had a welder down the street do that." He walks back over to the driver's side and opens the door. He turns the key in the new ignition switch, mounted under the dash, one notch to the right. I can hear the radiator fans turn on. "The fans turn on with the key," he says. "You got your turn signal," and he pushes the new shiny silver lever on the steering column up and down. "Hazards," he pulls the red lever on the signal switch. "Horn," he pushes a yellowed round button under the dash and the horn honks like a horn should honk. "I got the horn from Leon." He points to the floor board and a silver button you push with your foot. "There's your dimmer switch."

"How 'bout the wipers?" I ask, and Peanuts points to the round wiper switch on the top middle of the dash right below the windows. He turns it and the small wipers scrape the dusty dry windows back and forth.

"You got everything you need to make it legal," he assures me. Peanuts has also put the radiator hose on, the transmission cooler lines in, changed the alternator, and a handful of other miscellaneous engine things that had to be complete to make the car run.

"Put a few quarts of that tranny fluid in, and the gas in the can," he instructs me. I had bought a couple of plastic funnels at the store and walk to the other side of the car to empty everything in.

"All of it?" I ask when I get to the gas.

"All of it."

I walk back around and sit in the driver's seat. Peanuts is head first in the engine compartment.

"Have you driven it?" I call out to him.

He lifts his head towards me. "No, no. I was saving that for you!" he says. "Go ahead and turn the key."

I put my right foot on the brake instinctively, put my hand on the key, and turn it. The engine cranks. It backfires and a puff of dust or smoke blows out of the carburetor.

"Is that right?" I ask from inside the car.

"Yep. It's just been a while," he reassures me, and like all car guys vs. me, knows that what I think is certain failure, is just part of the process and totally fine. "Try it again."

I turn the key once more. Peanuts gives it gas with his hand on the accelerator cable. I try a third time and the '41, like an ancient machine, suddenly comes to life with sounds and colors.

There are a few more pops and bangs, which Peanuts describes as normal. He adjusts the idle to something that sounds calm and asks me to, "Put it into gear and see what happens."

I shift the car into drive, but it doesn't move at all. "Nothing," I call out to him. "It's in gear." I put the car back in park and Peanuts walks back to the passenger side to have a look. I put the car into drive a second time and nearly knock him over as the car jerks into drive and I slam on the brakes. I laugh out loud and he looks up and smiles at me.

"I'll open the gate," he says. "Back it out. See if she'll go."

It almost happens too quickly. Like I wasn't even ready for it. But that's what you do, I suppose, when you fix a car. You drive it.

And so just like that, Peanuts opens the gate, I put the car in reverse, back out of the driveway, put it in drive, and drive down the street.

I leave the car with Peanuts as he has a few things to adjust before I bring it home the next morning, which by a stroke of luck, cosmic timing, or just plain coincidence, happens to be October 8, 2012. A year to the day after my father died. Peanuts leaves the car on my trailer at Leon's, and I make the trip over the mountain once more, pay Leon for some parts, and Big Ray guides me out the gate, '41 in tow.

It's a beautiful El Paso afternoon with a clear blue sky and a breeze, not unlike three hundred other El Paso days in any given year. I let the '41 off the trailer and into the driveway and park the trailer on the street. There are still things left to do. Get a speedometer cable. Change the temperature gauge. Replace the starter. All important but seem, all of a sudden, to be just a formality.

I walk into my house and into the living room where I pick up the heavy box of my father's ashes that have been sitting on the mantle for the last year. I put them under one arm, run my fingers over my father's photograph, and walk back outside. I open the driver's door and wiggle into the seat, reaching over to set the ashes on the passenger side next to me.

I close the door, adjust the rearview, put my hand on the key, and start the car. I shift into drive and let go of the brakes. Then the engine turns the flywheel, which turns with the torque converter, which turns the transmission, which turns the drive shaft, which turns the rear end, which turns the wheels. Gravel crunches under the tires. The car moves forward. I turn left out of the driveway and into the street and after two-and-a-half often difficult, sometimes amazing years, I finally take my father for a ride in the '41.

Acknowledgments

My father for giving me a story to tell
Babette for being rock solid
Eddie Solis and John Attel for helping me achieve something
Eddie Okies for being a role model friend
Carlos and Willie for building our world
Doug for help in the hood
Leon for filling the gaps
Ernie for helping me stop
Peanuts for electrifying
Johnny por masa con fuerza
Uncle Bill, Vince, and Butch for laughing lunches
George Butterworth, Staci Brewster, John Harris, Kerrie Copelin and
the ALS Association of New Mexico
Linda, Evelyn, and Gabby from Choice Hospice
Linda and Gene Ott
Jen Nash
Jordan Powell
Miranda Lambert

Jeremy Gough for telling me to just write

My editor Jodi Egerton for nitpicking
but giving me confidence most of all

Joni Mulder, Rebecca Maizel, Libby Weaver, Monaca Brown, Lynda
Angelone, Stephanie Rios, Weiss Eubanks, Becky Ankeny

Dyer Auto Salvage, Ernie's Muffler and Brake, Chassis Engineering,
Inc., Emmit Radiator, The Filling Station, Nuts & Bolts of El Paso

My family and friends

And to the many thousands of ALS sufferers
who have a story I can't wait to hear

Please visit www.alsa.org for more information on ALS
and to join the fight for a cure

For more information, photographs, and proper thanks please visit
www.thefortyonebook.com

Made in the USA
Coppell, TX
02 June 2021

56758612R00163